The Vigil of PRAYER

Nolan P. Howington

BROADMAN PRESS
Nashville, Tennessee

Dedicated to
Marietta, whose love and
goodness have enriched my life beyond measure.

Unless otherwise stated, all Scripture quotations are from HOLY BIBLE, *New International Version,* copyright © 1978, New York Bible Society. Used by permission.
Scripture quotations marked KJV are from the King James Version of the Bible.

Library of Congress Cataloging-in-Publication Data

Howington, Nolan P.
  The vigil of prayer.

  1. Prayer. I. Title.
BV210.2.H68   1987   248.3'2   86-17181
ISBN 0-8054-1505-X (pbk.)

Contents

1

Wrestling with God
Genesis 32: 9-12, 24-32

Nothing so restores human usefulness as recovering one's faith in God. Dynamic faith is bound up with the practice of authentic prayer. "Christian prayer," wrote Georgia Harkness, "is prayer only when God meets man and man meets God in a living, personal encounter."[1]

Jacob, according to the Genesis story, apparently had quit praying. As a result, his consciousness of God had diminished. His spiritual life atrophied. For twenty years he had enjoyed material success, but he had drifted away from the Lord. Engrossed *with* things, he was too busy for God. Supported *by* things, he felt little need for God. Like the rich farmer in Jesus' parable (Luke 12:14-21), the accumulation of economic goods produced a false sense of security.

Biblical writers were honest. They made no apologies for the characters they portrayed. Jacob's faults and failures were faithfully delineated. He was a shady trickster, willing to lie and cheat, ready to exploit the weakness even of family members where that would advance his interests. How could God use such a person in His grand design? The late Sam Jones once said that there is some hickory too crooked even for God to work into an ax handle until He straightens out the stick.

God did indeed use Jacob but not until He worked some changes into his life. For Jacob it took a radical encounter with God, described in graphic oriental terms as *wrestling* with God.

Prayer: Provoked by Crisis

Jacob's abrupt action in departing Haran had stirred the anger of his Uncle Laban (Gen. 31:17-21). Jacob's twenty years in Haran had been

7

eventful for him. He had matched wits with the shrewd Laban. Laban appreciated the qualities of truthfulness and fidelity in others, though he never bothered to cultivate these traits in himself. He was no match, however, for his cunning nephew. In that contest between scoundrels, Jacob neatly swindled the older man's herds and flocks. Small wonder that he gathered up his family and possessions and stole silently away one night, hoping to escape Laban's wrath. Laban overtook Jacob in flight, but a divine warning prevented his planned reprisal. (Gen. 31:22-55). One crisis was averted, but an even more critical one awaited Jacob.

Esau, Jacob learned, was coming his way with a band of four-hundred men (Gen. 32:3-6). In great fear and distress, Jacob took what precautions he could against his brother's assault (Gen. 32:7-8). They were pathetically inadequate. At the end of his resources, Jacob resorted to prayer. Crisis often drives us to our knees when nothing else will. Jacob made his approach to God with a plea that God would honor his place in the covenant line and a divine promise made to him two decades earlier. For some reason we seem to think that God has a short memory, that He too easily forgets His promises.

Crisis is a time not to confront God but to look deep within your own soul. Jacob came to terms with himself as he waited in the divine presence. He confessed with full candor two powerful emotions:

First, he felt a sense of unworthiness. "I am unworthy of all the kindness and faithfulness you have shown your servant" (Gen. 32:10).[2] Was it his guilty conscience that prompted Jacob's prayer? After all, his past was cluttered with dishonesty, deception, and exploitation of others. His capacity for clever manipulation of persons and situations showed itself when he took advantage of Esau's appetite and purchased his twin brother's birthright for a bowl of lentil stew. Fresh from a fruitless hunting trip, and ravenous with hunger, Esau must have regarded that birthright as nearly worthless. "Look, I am about to die," Esau said. "What good is the birthright to me?" Jacob, the first in a long line of greedy food profiteers, capitalized on the weakness of a man governed by his stomach. The career in deceit was getting underway (Gen. 25:27-34).

Later, with help from his scheming mother, Jacob tricked his blind old father, receiving from him the paternal blessing reserved for the firstborn son. Poor dull-witted, sluggish-minded Esau might have been Isaac's favorite, but he was no match for Rebecca and the crafty Jacob. Blind, old, and fussy about his food, Isaac was deceived into granting the blessing that would establish Jacob, not Esau, as the head and priest of the clan. Jacob's fraud aroused a murderous intent in Esau's soul. The only salvation for Jacob was flight into exile (Gen. 27:1-45). Enroute to that exile in Haran, Jacob had a moving religious experience at Bethel (Gen. 28:10-22). With the passing of time, that experience dimmed and he slipped back into the patterns of deception and exploitation.

Now the threat of disaster faced Jacob with the coming of Esau. Reunion with his brother proved no joyful prospect! Over the years, the bitterness in Esau's soul had washed out, and his economic fortunes had brought satisfying success. But Jacob knew none of these developments. That is why he fawned rather sickeningly before his brother: "Your servant Jacob . . . my lord Esau" (Gen. 32:4,18). The situation facing this desperate man required more than a bribe or placating words.

Crisis is a time of sifting or separation. Crisis sometimes introduces grave peril fraught with judgment. It may also be a time of challenge and opportunity. For Jacob it was a crisis of conscience. Memory dredged up his past deeds. He felt the hot flush of shame and unworthiness as he prayed before Him who knows what we are and censures our bad motives and conduct. A person may reveal one self to the world and another to his own mind, but God sees him as he actually is. Genuine prayer allows no self-displays or false fronts. When we come before Him, we must be honest and open. "I am unworthy"—that must be our posture. Our wrestling confronts us with our sins.

Second, Jacob was gripped by a sense of fear. "Save me, I pray, from the hand of my brother Esau, for I am afraid" (Gen. 32:11). Neither Jacob's wealth, his cunning, nor his overriding confidence equipped him to handle the anxiety that tore at his soul. He could visualize the anger of his brother descending like a storm upon himself and his defenseless family. Because fears generally are compounded at night, the darkness at Jabbok kept alive the sense of helplessness reflected in his earlier prayer. That added to the intensity of his struggle (Gen. 32:24).

We may thrust guilt back into the subconscious mind, sweeping dirt under the rug for months or years. Invariably it returns to haunt us. All the old dreads returned to trouble Jacob. The truth of a biblical text, written much later, applied to him: "You may be sure that your sin will find you out" (Num. 32:23).

Cornered by conscience, none of Jacob's prized possessions could shield him. Like many persons who trust in wealth, he learned how vain and empty that can be when human life is at stake. Jacob feared Esau—and rightly so. But he needed to be fearing God, for only He can provide cleansing and reconciliation and make persons forgiving and brotherly. Jacob was destined to be a father in Israel and he had the potential for that role. But prior to Jabbok, he was not worthy. Like a diamond in the rough, Jacob needed cutting, shaping, and polishing. His troubles and his sense of guilt proved to be God's chastening rod—reducing his pride and increasing his humility.

Prayer: Sustained by Solitude

Our most genuine praying occurs when God alone is our audience. The great prayers of the Bible demonstrate this fact. "Jacob was left alone," we read, "and a man wrestled with him until daybreak" (Gen. 32:24). Despite the value of public or small-group prayer, our best praying is done by ourselves.

A. N. Whitehead once declared that religion is what we do with our solitude. For certain, solitude is the friend of true prayer. Reacting to ostentatious public prayers, Jesus counseled his followers to do their praying in private. "When you pray, go into your room, close the door and pray to your Father, who is unseen. Then your Father, who sees what is done in secret, will reward you" (Matt. 6:6). People who pray like that do not have to advertise their piety. They radiate a Presence and reflect a goodness born of communion with the Father.

In our rushed, hectic, urban life, we may have to plan our quiet times when we can be still and know that He is God (Ps. 46:10). This is a priority matter and an oft-neglected one. We sometimes argue that we do our praying as we drive to work, or we retreat into ourselves during the workday to engage in meditation. Such practices have value but often are subject to interruption and may degenerate into trivial exercises. There is no substitute for the planned, sustained rendezvous with God when we close the door to the world and commune with Him.

Moses was alone in the desert when he had his experience with God at the burning bush (Ex. 3:1-10). Jesus did some of his most fervent praying in the solitude of the desert or the garden of Gethsemane. Martin Luther's practice of rising early each morning to devote time to prayer was, by his own admission, necessitated by the demands of each day. For many of us, the early hours of the day afford the best opportunity to meditate and pray. Whatever time one chooses, the significant thing is aloneness before God.

The importance of this is apparent. Jesus appealed for prayers that are devoid of playacting and attempts to overwhelm God with excessive words (Matt. 6:6-7). The kind of praying we sometimes do publicly, marked by rhetoric and "purple passages" intended to impress people, is out of place in the prayer closet. At Jabbok and at Bethel, Jacob's life was totally exposed to the eye of God (Hos. 12:3-6). Similarly, our private prayers allow no defenses thrown up to cover our bad attitudes or unholy behavior. All that we are stands naked and open before His eye (Heb. 4:13). Confronted by the Holy One, we see ourselves for what we are. That may be the beginning of moral cleansing and a new direction (Isa. 6:1-8).

Persons who pray regularly know the significance of solitude. Life is so full of noise, commotion, and pagan appeals that ignore God or tune Him out altogether. Has it not always been that way? God's people have generally fought to keep faith fresh and the sense of the presence of God alive in their lives. Not just to survive spiritually but because of joy in the Lord, we welcome the loneliness of Jabbok, the stillness of a prayer room, the privacy of a wooded nook, or the office with its closed door.

America has hardly produced a more notable, Christlike person than Walter Rauschenbusch. Rauschenbusch has been maligned by critics who seem never to have read his works, especially his written prayers, or sensed the genuine piety and compassion of this godly man. The depth of his evangelical faith is reflected in "The Postern Gate," a poem he wrote in later life during a critical illness. These are the thoughts of a man who is looking death in the face.

> In the castle of my soul
> Is a little postern gate,
> Whereat, when I enter,
> I am in the presence of God.
> In a moment, in the turning of a thought,
> I am where God is.
> This is a fact.
>
> ....
>
> When I am with God
> I look deep down and high up,
> And all is changed.
> The world of men is made of jangling noises.
> With God is a great silence.
>
> ....
>
> When I enter into God,
> All life has a meaning.
> Without asking I know;
> My desires are even now fulfilled,
> My fever is gone
> In the great quiet of God.
>
> ....
>
> When I am in him, I am in the Kingdom of God
> And in the Fatherland of my Soul.[3]

Prayer: Marked by Struggle

Jacob learned what the saints have discovered: prayer can be like a wrestling match or a battlefield. "A man wrestled with him till daybreak. . . . you have struggled with God" (Gen. 32:24,28). Those words bespeak the intensity of the man's praying. The same kind of intensity is seen in Jesus' wilderness experience when He grappled with the issue of His life purpose and the strategy required for implementing that purpose (Matt. 4:1-11). This is seen also in the agonizing experience in Gethsemane when He faced the reality of the cross (Matt. 26:36-46). Prayer as wrestling with God was a familiar experience for the apostle Paul, especially intercessory prayer (Rom. 15:30-31; Col. 4:12-13).

Praying can be hard work. George Mueller knew that as he daily cried out to God for his orphans, depending on the prayer of faith to meet the needs of those children. Charles Spurgeon learned from Mueller that a man must maintain a prayer vigil, for this keeps the channel open for the flowing of the divine gifts. A man of great faith, Spurgeon depended on prayer for the meeting of financial and spiritual needs. He never used high-pressure methods to raise money. A group of his members met in a room beneath the sanctuary to pray while Spurgeon preached. "The prayer of a righteous man is powerful and effective" (Jas. 5:16).

None of this means that God is reluctant to grant our needs or that He can be won over by verbal barrages. The prophets of Baal hopped up and down and shouted until exhausted, but no fire fell. But the fervor and faith of an Elijah gained an answer from God. Fisher Humphreys was on target when he defined prayer as "talking to God who listens to us and responds to us because he loves us."[4] We do not thus wrestle *against* God but *with* Him. The outcome of our prayer brings changes in us, not in Him.

The most fervent prayer allows no trespassing of God's domain. True, Jesus Christ has opened for us a welcomed access to the Father (Heb. 4:14-16; 10:19-22). But our approach to God must always be in reverence and humility. He is holy and sovereign; we are unclean and finite. God has a right to our name, as Jacob learned, but is under no obligation to reveal His own (Gen. 32:27-29). In the ancient world, the notion existed that a person's self was concentrated in the person's name. Jacob's antagonist retained His name; Jacob could not therefore gain power over Him. In our prayer struggles, the difference between God and humanity is not blotted out. He remains sovereign even when He shows mercy. We remain His subjects, dependent on that mercy.

Intensive prayer can be painful. Jacob's encounter with God marked a turning point in his life. He came to that experience as a beseiged soul facing a crisis he could not handle. The encounter was costly, resulting in a wrenched hip (Gen 32:25) and the surrender of his identity as a deceiver who lived by his wits. In receiving a new name and a new nature,

Jacob was remade spiritually. "Your name will no longer be Jacob, but Israel, because you have struggled with God and with men and have overcome. . . . Then he blessed him there" (32:28-29).

People who pray for the will of God, the revelation of His purpose, must be ready to accept the answer when it comes. The shape of obedience to the divine will may mean radical changes or unexpected courses of action. When William Carey led Drury Lane to pray for foreign missions, God called Carey himself to go out as a missionary to Burma. That is one way for a church to get rid of a pastor! Little did Saul of Tarsus know what God's answer would be when he asked, "What shall I do, Lord?" (Acts 22:10). The way Saul traveled in fulfilling God's mission for his life was full of achievements marked by peril and pain. Divine grace is costly, never cheap. The same may be true of the obedience God requires.

Prayer may mean a lonely and agonizing struggle. But when it produces a new person fit for God's purposes, it is eminently worthwhile.

Prayer: Strengthened by Persistence

A persistent person holds doggedly to an idea or a course of action adjudged worthy of time and energy. Jacob was like that. He persisted in prayer throughout the night (Gen. 32:24), hanging on till the answer came.

(1) Persistence means keeping a regular pattern of prayer. Prayer is a viable and time-honored practice, an essential element in the religious life. For that reason we are enjoined to pray regularly (Luke 18:1; 1 Thess. 5:17). Failing to pray is a sin of omission (1 Sam. 12:23). Prayer stimulates spiritual growth. It helps God do His work in the world.

(2) Persistence often applies to the duration of our prayers. The severity of the problem or the acuteness of the need may detain us for lengthy periods. This was true of Jacob. This also was Jesus' practice when situations required it. The average Christian seldom remains at prayer for hours at a time and need not feel guilty about it. The length of our prayers is not as significant as their genuineness or the habitual openness of our lives toward God. Nonetheless, the child of God may occasionally need the extended vigil.

(3) Persistence means steadfast devotion to those concerns dear to the heart of God. A deepening fellowship with the Father leads us to an understanding of His mind and the things He desires for His creation. Maturity of soul is born of this intimate relationship with God, not from infrequent and sporadic seasons of prayer.

Persistence in prayer enables us increasingly to accept the wisdom of God for our lives. We become less like little children who ply parents with requests until they give in. Persistence calls for patience, the assurance that God hears our prayers and that He will make a fitting response to them. Some persons may argue that we always get answers provided the common hindrances are removed: lack of faith, the presence of sin, bitterness, improper motive, or a bad spirit. Obviously, these are obstacles to effective prayer, but their removal brings no automatic answers to our prayers. God cannot be manipulated even by our goodness!

Divine wisdom denies some requests and delays the answer to others. Some of the delays are purposeful either because we are not ready for the answer or because He wishes to confer a greater benefit upon us. This aspect of the divine nature is seen in the death and raising of Lazarus. When Jesus received word from Bethany that Lazarus was critically ill, He delayed His trip two whole days. That delay gave Him opportunity to perform a greater ministry both for His disciples and for the sisters (John 11:4-44). In asserting His mastery over life and death, He quickened their faith and that of many Jews (11:45).

Sustained prayer ensures us against impatience or faith loss when God seems to move slowly. Perhaps this is the meaning of Jesus' story about an insistent widow and a heartless judge (Luke 18:1-8). This story deals in contrasts. God is not like that annoyed judge, for He listens patiently to our prayers and will answer them, often in surprising ways (18:8). Jesus puts a premium also upon continual prayer, for it witnesses to our confidence in a faithful Father.

Authentic prayer is never a failure. Jacob met with a denial but received the kind of help he really needed (Gen. 32:29). God gave him inner fortification and courage enough to meet Esau. He left Jabbok in humility and gratitude, a totally changed person.

The strength of Jacob's encounter with God evidently kept him on track thereafter. He carried that experience in his heart until the day of his death. The crisis in his soul at Jabbok caused him to fling his life in desperation upon the mercies of God. Life was never again the same for him.

> From strength to strength go on,
> Wrestle and fight and pray;
> Tread all the powers of darkness down,
> And win the well-fought day.

2

An Honest Confession
Psalm 32

Speaking to a convocation at Southern Baptist Seminary, theologian Albert Outler advised preachers to stick to the basics. "People both desire and need to hear about God and forgiveness of sin," Outler declared. Proclamation that offers a way out of our moral blundering and release from our guilt finds a responsive audience.

How desperate is the human situation? Our top law-enforcement agency regularly posts a list of prominent criminals judged to be a special menace to society. Why are these persons such a threat? Is it not because they have no regard for human life, moral restraints, or even God Himself? They belong in the category of super sinners. But, in all honesty, the sin so prominent in their lives to some degree appears in us, also.

If we take the biblical teaching seriously, the number-one problem of our society is *sin,* the moral fault or tragic flaw permeating life and producing a multiplicity of *sins.* This evil in us is as old as Adam. It comes with each generation and must be handled by every person. How are we to deal with it?

The writer of Psalm 32, out of his own experience, provided an answer. An honest confession, he declared, opens the way to the deliverance we seek (v. 5). He described the guilt that makes confession imperative, the problem associated with confession, and the gratifying release that follows full confession.

Guilt's Underlying Causes

An honest confession faces up to the fact of guilt and its underlying causes. Tradition associates Psalm 32 with King David. What is certain

is the writer's authentic religious experience. He described no hypotheti-
cal or imaginary situation. This psalm reflects events and emotions
drawn from his own life. It takes us back of the writer's guilt feelings and
suggests some of the factors that impelled confession. We identify with
his experience because guilt troubles us for the same reasons.

1. Guilt occurs when we transgress the bounds of our moral nature.
Made in the image of God, we possess a moral faculty that enables us
to discern right and wrong. Conscience is a part of our moral endow-
ment. Its content obviously depends largely on the kind of training we
have received. A conscience instructed by the Bible, sensitized by prayer,
and directed by the Spirit of God is a valuable guide, though not infalli-
ble. It will sound the alarm when we misuse our God-given freedom and
violate our moral nature.

I once heard a lecturer advise his audience, "Train up a conscience in
the way it should go, and when you are old it will not embarrass you."
Conscience is not the voice of God, but it surely is more than a human
voice. Properly formed, conscience helps us keep faith with the divine
purpose for our lives. Failure to regard that purpose is sin. Sin is "missing
the mark" (*hatta'h*), being guilty of moral failure, especially toward God
(Lam. 5:7; Ps. 32:1,5; 51:4).

2. Guilt often follows violations of God's moral law. One Old Testament term for such violations is *pesha,* "transgressions" (Ps. 32:1,5). This
refers to sustained rebellion, not temporary moral lapses such as Paul
described in Galatians 6:1. The earliest example of this attempt to throw
off divine restraints is found in Genesis 3. Adam and Eve disobeyed
God's command, seeking freedom but finding only pain and guilt. Similarly, David's adulterous relationship with Bathsheba was followed by
an appalling sense of guilt (2 Sam. 11—12). Guilt can be so oppressive
as to create inward distress, health imbalance, or even self-destruction
(Matt. 27:3-5).

Sin is a form of anarchy. It shows a person's will to live by the laws
of his or her own choosing. This means a disregard or open rejection of
the moral law established by God. Essentially, it is a rejection of God
Himself, a repudiation of both the law and the Lawgiver. We have an
example of this truth in the New Testament. Love, so Jesus teaches, is

the guiding principle for His followers. Love is to govern their relationships toward both believers and nonbelievers (John 13:34-35; 14:15; 15:9-17). Infractions of that central imperative are a repudiation of Him who gave the directive (Matt. 25:41-45).

Happy is the person who feels a sense of guilt for having transgressed the moral law! There is hope for a soul disturbed about rebellion and seeking divine forgiveness.

3. Guilt occurs when we bury sins rather than confess them. Biblical passages like Psalm 32 reveal a variety of terms used to describe breaches of moral righteousness. "Iniquity" (*awon*) and "deceit" (*rami 'ah*) designate a category of wrongdoing we sometimes endeavor to conceal. The list is broad: lust, greed, pride, hatred, jealousy, envy, sloth, lying, failure to do good, and perversion of legitimate desires (Isa. 1:4-6,15-20; Matt. 5:22,28; Mark 7:20-23; Rom. 12:14-21; Gal. 5:19-21; Eph. 4:25-31; Col. 3:5-10; Jas. 4:17; and 1 John 4:20-21).

Deceit, so W. R. Taylor reminded us, includes self-deception. It is the means by which we try to excuse or palliate offenses, build our rationalizations, and so evade the obligation to clear ourselves of guilt.[1] We wish to appear better than we are but lack the will to surrender the sins that block authentic goodness. The human mind is quite adept at rationalizing and covering up guilt. For that reason, the best of us need often to pray,

> Search me, O God, and know my heart;
> test me and know my anxious thoughts.
> See if there is any offensive way in me,
> and lead me in the way everlasting (Ps. 139:23-24).

Our way of covering sins produces guilt (Ps. 32:3-4); *God's* way of covering them produces blessedness (32:1).

Problems Associated with Confession

E. Stanley Jones, missionary to India, told of a young Hindu who boasted of membership in a Society for the Confession of Sin. The Christian missionary congratulated him and then asked, "Isn't it hard for you to confess your sins to one another?" The youth replied, "We confess other people's sins, not our own!" That, I suspect, is a rather large society and is not limited to India.

1. One problem preventing confession is a reluctance to own up to our misdeeds or our unchristian spirit. Pride blocks any disposition to honest admission of our inner weakness and our poor performances. Our sinful self finds ways to justify our behavior or to cover up our guilt. Perhaps that is why William Temple charged that a sinful self could never save itself!

We sometimes shift blame for our sins onto society, our ancestors, the local situation, or the circumstances confronting us. On occasion we blame the devil or our own fleshly weaknesses as though we were helpless before these. A three-year-old had just torn a valuable document to shreds and was being sharply scolded by an angry father. "Why on earth did you do that?" he shouted. Fearful, the little fellow replied, "Daddy, I was just standing there. That paper was in my hands. All at once my hands started tearing it up. I don't know why they did it!" That is pretty good for a small child. It is not unlike the guilt dismissal practiced by some adults.

2. An easygoing attitude toward sin makes confession seem irrelevant or unnecessary. Biblical standards of morality suffer in the marketplace, are challenged by modern advertising and some forms of entertainment, and seem to be abandoned totally by groups that promote unchristian life-styles. Tolerance toward sinful pursuits invades the church itself. A church member recently expressed appreciation for our "open society." "People are so much more lenient and broad-minded these days," she said. "Even our preachers show more understanding and tolerance about the things people do."

Broad-mindedness can be only an easygoing attitude toward evil. Is it broad-minded to overlook the damaging impact of alcohol and drugs on persons? Does charitableness include an acceptance of pornography, sexual immorality in its varied forms, racism, economic injustice, gambling, and the exploitation of the poor? The sincere child of God weighs conduct and human relationships on the scales of Scripture. Love never includes an acceptance of things that limit or hurt persons.

3. Confession comes hard for persons who are unwilling to bare their

souls, even to God. An alcoholic and a minister were kneeling in prayer. "Lord," the pastor prayed, "help this poor drunkard." The man broke in, protestingly. "Don't tell Him I'm a drunkard; tell Him I'm sick!" It is difficult for us to look our sin in the face and acknowledge it for what it is.

Confession is our admission of personal inadequacy in the face of a hard task, a serious trouble, or a past misdeed. Generally, confession is an acknowledgment of sin and guilt. Even when we are desperately hurting, it seems difficult for us to muster courage enough to declare any sin in another's presence. Public confessions are even more difficult.

Why are we so slow to open our hearts to a trusted friend, a competent pastor, or even to our Father God? One reason may be the historic Protestant criticism of Roman Catholic confessional practices and a concurrent feeling that confession, if made at all, should be a private matter between the individual and God. This overlooks the biblical injunction, "Confess your sins to each other and pray for each other" (Jas. 5:16). Another reason may be the fear of human reactions to our confession. One person remarked, "My pastor is a godly man, and he has a good opinion of me. I could never talk to him about my problems. Besides, I would feel like a human target later if he publicly dealt with such sins."

That woman's attitude sounds rather immature, almost silly. Suppose a person refused to have dinner with a physician who had once operated on him. He might reason, "Why, that man knows all about my insides. Even as we eat, he can visualize how they are behaving. I would be embarrassed to death to sit down with him at a dinner table!"

Certainly, there is no need to feel strange on entering the confessional when only God hears your voice. Does He not know His children fully, and has He not invited them into this sort of relationship? Before Him, pride and timidity can be set aside so that His healing mercies may work.

Failure to confess our sins to God produces disastrous results in our lives.

> When I kept silent,
> my bones wasted away

through my groaning all day long.
For day and night
your hand was heavy upon me;
my strength was sapped
as in the heat of summer (Ps. 32:3-4).

The consciousness of guilt may be suppressed, like dirt swept under a rug. Tucked back within the mind, it festers, boils, and irritates. It is like an unclean wound that never heals. Nervous tension, depression, anxiety, and even bodily illnesses often stem from this poison within the soul. The psalmist's description of his physical and emotional distress reads like the pages of a journal devoted to psychosomatic medicine.

Great novelists like Fedor Dostoyevsky (*Crime and Punishment*) and Nathaniel Hawthorne (*The Scarlet Letter*) portrayed the effects of unconfessed sin and the personal disturbances that follow the suppression of guilt. Pastoral counselors and psychiatrists know that sins buried deep within the self cause conflicts and play havoc with health of body and mind. A person in that condition fits James's description, "a double-minded man, unstable in all he does" (Jas. 1:8). He is a perpetual civil war. The lack of confession, like bottled steam, creates pressure and may cause an explosion.

Persons living with unconfessed sin are not unlike a group of small boys who were trapping yellow jackets in a glass bottle. The boys, led by a lad called Andrew, found a nest in a red clay bank. Andrew thrust the bottle into the opening. The disturbed insects quickly filled the bottle, delighting the boys who watched their frantic movements. Yellow jackets, however, are not always home. Those that had been on the wing returned while the boys were enjoying the show. They angrily attacked the youngsters and scattered them in all directions. Only Andrew was left, and they went to work on him. He could not drop the bottle with its angry residents, nor could he protect himself against their cousins. He could only cry pathetically, "Somebody come help me turn this bottle loose!" Is that not descriptive of persons needing the therapy of confession but unwilling to submit to it?

Confession's Welcome Release

What evokes the prayer of confession? Is it not a vision of the Holy One whom we have offended and our own desperate need for forgiveness (Isa. 6:5)? The man who wrote Psalm 32 recognized his offense. He realized something else: his inward torture was really the heavy hand of God pushing him toward divine mercy (Ps. 32:4). That discovery opened the way for healing. An ancient Hebrew prophet learned the same truth about God's dealings with individuals. "Come, let us return to the Lord./He has torn us to pieces/but he will heal us;/he has injured us/but he will bind up our wounds" (Hos. 6:1).

Aristotle once spoke of the power of drama to produce *catharsis* of the emotions. Well, for us it is sincere confession that relieves our troubled souls. "An honest confession is good for the soul" provided it is directed toward God. We can count on the Father's disposition to "forgive us our sins and purify us from all unrighteousness" (1 John 1:9).

A young woman came to talk with her pastor about some problems threatening her marriage. Her husband's profession occupied the bulk of his time. Due to his sterility, they had no children, and she found herself lonely and bored with life. She confessed to a series of premarital sex experiences and to one affair with another man after her marriage. Eventually, her earlier Christian training caught up with her, and her sense of guilt became unbearable. One evening she had unburdened her soul to her husband but had gotten no help from him. Now with the pastor's help, she confessed to God. It was then that the guilt was absolved, and she found the peace of mind she had long sought.

Confession in that person's case was coupled with repentance, the will to turn life about and to walk in a new direction. There is a blessedness that comes when God removes sins from our lives. The psalmist exulted in the power that had forgiven his transgressions and so covered them that they became invisible even to God (Ps. 32:1). We, too, know about sins being hidden, covered by the blood of the Lamb. God in Christ has forgiven us "once for all" (Heb. 9:14,26; 1 Pet. 1:18-21). Like the psalmist, we know the joy of being delivered, reconciled, and at peace with God

(Ps. 32:7). The old record that stood against us has been erased. God alone can bring that off.

William Shakespeare's drama *The Tragedy of Macbeth* is an excellent study in the search for release from the torture of guilt. At one point Macbeth questioned a physician:

> Canst thou not minister to a mind diseased,
> Pluck from the memory a rooted sorrow,
> Raze out the written troubles of the brain,
> And with some sweet oblivious antidote
> Cleanse the stuff'd bosom of that perilous stuff
> Which weighs upon the heart?[2]

The answer to that is no. But there is a Great Physician who can work that change in us.

> There is a fountain filled with blood
> Drawn from Immanuel's veins;
> And sinners, plunged beneath that flood,
> Lose all their guilty stains.

For the psalmist, the experience of forgiving love instilled in his heart a flood of joy similar to the burst of flowers under the magic of sunlight (Ps. 32:11). His experience gave rise not only to a grateful testimony but to instructions for persons seeking a better way (32:6-10). The twin emotions of joy and gratitude are inevitable notes in the song of deliverance.

3

The Way Back to God
Psalm 51: 1-17

Late one evening, a jangling telephone interrupted my studies. The anxious voice of a person unknown to me blurted out a question: "Does God forgive us all our sins?" Then the woman launched into a story that threw light on her question. She had a position with a local firm that involved handling considerable sums of money each week. Under normal circumstances, her salary would have been adequate. But her husband's lengthy illness left the family's support dependent on her earnings. Two years before that time, her small son had broken his neck, and the family was still paying off the medical expenses. In addition, the woman was helping to support a disabled father.

Caught up in this financial crunch, she had resorted to embezzling company funds. Said she, "I rationalized this deed, hid the evidence, and hoped somehow to return the money before the theft was detected. What I have done is wrecking my life, taking my appetite, and robbing me of sleep or normal relations with my family. I am ready to confess my stealing and try to make restitution. But my biggest problem is my disturbed conscience. I have been a Christian a long time, and I know I have offended God. I am guilty! Tell me, will God forgive me this sin?"

Several passages of Scripture came to mind that applied to the caller's condition. The one that proved most helpful was Psalm 51. This bit of sacred writing speaks to any person who feels adrift in a sea of guilt and sin. The most penitential piece of literature in existence, it contains the soulful cry of a guilty person who is battling his way back to God. The psalm is the intensely personal, coming up out of a broken heart. It penetrates our own consciousness, for in some ways the psalmist's moral dilemma is ours as well. We share his sense of sin and his longing for moral renewal. We learn from his experience what the pattern of restoration requires.

A Contrite Spirit

Contrition is the honest acknowledgment of one's sin and the sincere desire for divine forgiveness. The path to contrition unfolds in the experience of the psalmist. From this man we learn that God uses many avenues to bring us both to sense and to admit the guilt in our souls. We discover that sin can neither be hidden nor denied. For sensitive souls, realizing the full impact of sin, must accept responsibility for their misdeeds. Knowing that sin is directed toward God and that the sinner deserves punishment, they are brought to a crushed and broken condition.

The spirit of contrition is not commonplace in contemporary culture. Karl Menninger, a clinical psychiatrist, wrote a book entitled *Whatever Became of Sin?* Anyone who observes human behavior or follows the news knows that sin has neither vanished nor lost its hold on persons. Menninger knew that quite well. His probing question deals with the loss of a sin consciousness, the easygoing view of immorality in general.

Such a relaxed view of evil and guilt stems in part from a loss of God consciousness and a repudiation of the moral order which He has established. Disdain for God and a ruling morality is reflected in such modern expressions as "If it feels good, it's good," "doing what comes naturally," or "doing my own thing." We have popularized an ancient Greek philosopher's claim that "Man is the measure of all things" or the biblical statement: "Every man did that which was right in his own eyes" (Judg. 17:6; 21:25, KJV). That kind of living brings moral anarchy and chaos. We live in a universe couched in moral law, by design of the Creator. We ignore or violate God's moral demands at our own peril.

Unlike the beasts of the field, men and women are reflective, moral creatures. As such, they are subject to the divine law which is the norm for their decisions and conduct. The writer of Psalm 51 had transgressed the bounds of his own moral nature and the moral will of God. A long-standing tradition identifies the writer as King David, whose lust, adultery, and intrigue leading to murder had provoked the wrath of God (see 2 Sam. 11—12). This tradition, so an Old Testament scholar notes, can neither be proved nor disproved.[1] But the content of the psalm fits David's experience.

The consciousness of sin grows out of the awareness that one has violated the laws and purposes of a holy God. In David's case, lust and covetousness led to adultery, the disruption of another family, and the death of his paramour's husband. After describing the reprehensible behavior of the king and his lover, the biblical writer noted, "But the thing David had done displeased the Lord" (2 Sam. 11:27). That little line, with its evaluation of human conduct, never appears at the end of those sexual escapades dramatized on television and movie screens or the sensual scenes described in modern novels.

The consciousness of wrongdoing may be brought on by various means as David's life illustrates. It may come from the prophetic word of God: "You are the man!" (2 Sam. 12:7). It may be stirred by the crisis of illness and death or by the suffering of the innocent and the survival of the guilty (2 Sam. 12:13-19). Again, it may be caused by the direct probing of the Holy Spirit and the awareness that His absence from life would result in a hopeless state (Ps. 51:11). All of these proved to be God's barbed arrow in the psalmist's soul, leading to a conviction of sin and an open admission of guilt.

Within this psalm is no excuse for past behavior, no attempt to gloss over guilt. "I know my transgressions,/and my sin is always before me" (51:3). There is no attempt to blame ancestors or to plead extenuating circumstances. The psalmist saw and accepted responsibility for his actions. From birth he had lived with sinning tendencies (51:5), a fact true of us as well (Rom. 3:23). A sense of inner honesty, however, led him to accept blame rather than pass it along to others.

An elderly deacon had the habit of greeting his pastor's sermon with the self-righteous remark, "Preacher, you really laid it into them today!" Though prone to profanity and stinginess, he never applied the preached Word to himself. One Sunday the young preacher kept emphasizing the relevance of the gospel to every person present. He kept saying, "This message is for you—*every one* of you!" That day, the old deacon greeted his pastor sheepishly, saying, "Preacher, you really laid it into *us* today!" From that day he used a rake to draw the sermon to himself rather than a shovel to throw the message over his shoulder upon others.

Admission of our guilt includes the awareness that ultimately sin is directed against God Himself and that the sinner deserves to be punished (Ps. 51:4b). Sin is a part of the perennial human revolt against the authority of God. "Against you, you only, have I sinned/and done what is evil in your sight" (51:4). Obviously, our sin is damaging to self and to others touched by it. But our offenses against persons are also directed against God, even as our loving care for persons reflects our love for Him (Matt. 25:37-45). God had crushed this poor man and left him devoid of joy (51:8). Out of this desperate condition he pleaded for mercy and cleansing (51:1-2,7,9-10). He counted on God's unfailing love and great compassion (51:1), offering God nothing more than a broken and con-trite heart (51:17).

> The tumult and the shouting dies,
> The captains and the kings depart—
> Still stands thine ancient sacrifice,
> A broken and a contrite heart.[2]

A Steadfast Spirit

The life restored to fellowship with God needed a permanent anchorage. Anxious to stay on track, the psalmist begged God to renew a steadfast spirit within him (51:10). Steadfastness in this case meant a faithful adherence to God's moral demands especially as found in Israel's cove-nant relationship with Him (Ps. 78:8,37; Hos. 4:1-3-6a). This man want-ed forgiveness and cleansing; he also wanted stability and continuity in living uprightly. We can ask no less for our own lives.

Steadfastness is born of commitment, and commitment to the lordship of Jesus Christ is at the heart of the Christian life (Rom. 10:9-10). This is implicit within the act of baptism itself. To be immersed into the name of the Father, Son, and Holy Spirit (Matt. 28:19) suggests a dedication of life to all that the Triune God requires of us. The early church accepted responsibility for establishing new converts in their newfound faith. Following baptism, these converts "devoted themselves to the apostles' teaching and to the fellowship, to the breaking of bread and to prayer" (Acts 2:42). This way of handling newborn Christians, sometimes called "front-door discipline," confirmed in them the notion that they were called to unremitting loyalty to Christ.

Sadly, some church members demonstrate no such commitment to Christ. They lack stability, having left their first love (Rev. 2:4) or having settled down to a lukewarm churchianity (Rev. 3:16). Fickleness among Jesus' followers has been a problem from the beginning of the Christian movement (John 6:60-66).

Years ago in a rural church revival, I encountered several cases of chronic instability within the membership. During the week we had an unusual number of people asking for rebaptism. I discovered that some of these persons had already been baptized more than once. On Sunday, the final day of the revival, we had dinner with an elderly couple. The housewife was a frank and outspoken person. Among other things she critically appraised the revival, especially the parade of persons presented for baptism. Said she, "They get religion on the installment plan, a little each August. Then they backslide for the rest of the year." Turning to me, she advised, "When you go down to that farm pond for the baptizing this afternoon, here's what you ought to do. Stand on the bank with a big flat rock in your hand. When the pastor finishes baptizing them, bash their heads in and send them on to glory. If their feet ever touch dry ground, they'll start backsliding right away!"

Needless to say, I did not follow her instructions, but I saw her point. From the beginning of the Christian life, there must be a fidelity to Christ and a steadfast commitment to that task which He assigned His people. There are specific ways in which this steadfastness takes shape:

(1) There is a development of Christian character and a loyal devotion to those things that are morally right and productive of goodness (2 Pet. 1:3-11). Christians are inwardly motivated by the Spirit who dwells within. One mark of maturity is the increasing desire for righteousness. Accordingly, we frequently and wisely pray, "Teach me to do your will,/for you are my God;/may your good Spirit/lead me on level

ground" (Ps. 143:10). The presence of the Spirit keeps us on track and gives us courage to obey the divine decrees (Ezek. 36:27).

(2) The Christian comes to hate and to resist evil. Any easygoing toleration of evil by the pulpit or the pew is playing into Satan's hands and encouraging the spread of wickedness. Because of the mystery of iniquity that works overtime, we are urged to pray, "Lead us not into temptation,/but deliver us from the evil one" (Matt. 6:13). Sensitive to his own propensity for evil, a devout soul implored God, "Let not my heart be drawn to what is evil,/to take part in wicked deeds/with men who are evildoers;/let me not eat of their delicacies" (Ps. 141:4). Our warfare with evil is unrelenting.

(3) Steadfastness takes shape as we learn to commit ourselves to the work of our Lord. Paul linked this quality with the believer's relationship to the risen Christ. He admonished Christians to "stand firm. Let nothing move you. Always give yourselves fully to the work of the Lord, because you know that your labor in the Lord is not in vain" (1 Cor. 15:58). "The work of the Lord" is an all-inclusive term that must not be given a restricted meaning. Let us examine the loyalty we owe the church—the church family to which we belong. That local body of believers is devoted to a ministry and mission given by Christ. Within that group of fellow Christians we find opportunity for growth, the worship of God, the sharing of a common witness, and a worldwide ministry. No person who claims to be in Christ can ignore or demean membership in His body. Devotion to Christ leads us to a steadfast loyalty to the church, its worship, and its work. Any person who, without good reason, habitually disregards responsible membership and faithful participation in the life of the church must answer to the Lord of the church (see Heb. 10:19-31).

A Consecrated Spirit

The prayer for forgiveness and steadfastness was followed by the plea for "a willing spirit" (Ps. 51:12) or an obedient spirit. Life nourished and sustained by God knows both joy and freedom.

One result of forgiveness and inner renewal is the recovery of a lost moral influence. Persons who lead public lives as King David did wield an influence for good or evil. David's multiple transgressions set forces in motion that disrupted his own household, shook a nation's confidence in his integrity, and led the Lord's enemies to view Him with contempt (2 Sam. 12:7-14). Nothing seems so damaging as a good man's retreat from goodness into a life of wrongdoing.

Once while visiting a hospitalized church member, I learned about such a person. When I entered a certain woman's room, I found her weeping. "The pain must be severe," I said. "Pastor, it's not bodily pain but the hurt inside." She had just been visited by her sister's husband who had once been a deacon and Sunday school leader in his church. Remembering how fervently he could pray, she asked him to offer up a prayer for her. Said she, "He blushed and blurted out the words, 'I can't do it. I don't pray, anymore.' "

For several months this man had moved in a direction away from God. Having located in another part of the city, he had engaged in business practices forbidden by his church, had felt the pull of greed, and had drifted away from the values he once cherished. Once useful to God and devoted to his church, he had lost all influence for good.

Every life casts a shadow. No person is without some kind of influence. Influence for the Christian is an active force, not a passive one. We put our influence to work for Christ. Jesus Christ incarnate in us makes His impact on people around us.

> Jesus shut within a book
> Is hardly worth a passing look.
> Jesus prisoned in a creed
> Is a fruitless Lord, indeed.
> But Jesus in the hearts of men
> Shows his tenderness again.

Forgiveness and restoration are not for mere selfish enjoyment. The rescued person goes to work to rescue others. "Then I will teach transgressors your ways,/and sinners will turn back to you" (Ps. 51:13). Such a person does not have to be pressured into Christian witnessing. He takes the initiative in reaching out to teach and guide others to the love that lifted him. God has removed the button from his tongue, and he sings aloud of the divine righteousness (51:14). Deliverance impels witnessing; witnessing follows deliverance.

Religious enthusiasm runs highest right after the experience of conversion or rescue from "years in sinning wasted." A person's circle of lost or spiritually blighted acquaintances may never be so large again. This is a strategic time to share one's experience with those friends. Should this not be done humbly and courteously (1 Pet. 3:15), in such fashion that the transgressor is left standing face-to-face with God? The witness shares his story about the lifting power of mercy and love (Ps. 51:1). Sinners are converted, however, not through our testimonies but through the graciousness of God.

Telling one's conversion experiences should throw the spotlight on the saving goodness of God, not on the storyteller. A dramatic presentation of a lurid, sinful background is legitimate only when it leaves the focus on God's redeeming love, not on the sordid deeds of the person involved. The object of witnessing should be obvious: "Sinners will turn back to you" (Ps. 51:13).

You can readily see why Psalm 51 provides a fitting answer to the question: "Does God forgive us all our sins?" He assuredly does when we acknowledge our guilt, accept responsibility for our deeds, and throw ourselves upon His mercy. The testimony of Scripture is that God loves us even in our waywardness. And "If we confess our sins, he is faithful and just and will forgive us our sins and purify us from all unrighteousness" (1 John 1:9).

4
Crisis at Mid-Life
Isaiah 38: 1-20

The word *crisis* does not appear in the pages of Scripture. Crisis experiences, however, are common occurrences for biblical personalities. Some wag, describing the exit of the first pair from Eden, has Adam saying to Eve, "My dear, I think we are entering upon a crisis." Noah's settled life was interrupted by the command to build an ark and ride out a flood. Abraham left his native land for an unknown country. That move, occurring at his life's midpoint, must have had a jarring impact on him and his wife. Moses, with two thirds of his life before him, went out from Pharoah's court into a desert experience. He probably wondered why God's call to lead Israel included forty years of sheepherding. Solomon's life was corrupted by materialism and sensuality, leaving him vulnerable to apostasy and idolatry. *Ecclesiastes,* whether or not written by him, certainly reflects the disillusionment and cynicism that attended his bitter experience.

Simon Peter faced the crisis of failure, but he handled it better than Judas who settled for a hangman's noose. Paul lived with one crisis after another, beginning, it seems, at the time he found new life in Christ. Demas could not handle crisis, so he abandoned faith and the Christian fellowship. *Hebrews* describes a parade of godly souls who found in life's critical junctures that an unbreakable faith in God was their one hope.

Crisis, so the Bible assures us, is a reality in human life. The experience of an Israelite king, himself about forty years old, provides helpful hints for crisis laden persons, especially those confronted by mid-life crises.

Reminder of Mortality

When crises stalk our lives during prime time (Isa. 38:10), they create stress and send shock waves through our whole system. Few persons in our culture escape some form of mid-life crisis attended by anxieties about aging and death and questions as to the meaning and purpose of existence. This experience sometimes is termed *middlescence* or *neoadolescence*. The critical years may vary, though the period from thirty-five to forty-five is most suspect.

Life's middle time brings an awareness of biological changes. These include the decline of vital powers, the alteration of sex drives, and the visible signs of aging. Along with these are possible modifications of the family pattern: the empty-nest syndrome, the wife's career demands, the reassessment of the husband-wife relationship, sexual infidelity, divorce, or residential change to fit the diminished family.

Biological and domestic changes do not fully account for a mid-life crisis. Underlying the crisis and feeding it are psychological stresses that are often bewildering and disturbing. A woman realizes that her youth is receding. Her childbearing days have ended, and the children for whom she lived are now gone. The husband of her youth now seems a stranger. A man begins to question his vocation and his achievements to date. He has anxieties about his diminished sex drives or the lack of rapport with his wife. His dreams of wealth and life goals have faded before harsh daily realities. He becomes like a person who arrives at the airport in time to see his flight departing!

The literature about mid-life crisis is filled with testimonies of persons harried by anxiety, fear, depression, emptiness, the "naked horror" of loneliness, and the diversion of energies to nonproductive pursuits. According to Carl Jung, about three fourths of our energy, which should go into fruitful work, is locked up in interior conflicts.[1] This is especially true of persons caught up in mid-life crises.

The real issue in a mid-life crisis is a spiritual one, a question about values, directions for the years ahead, a consciousness of mortality, and the haunting fear of death. Because we are reflective beings, more than galvanized flesh driven by insatiable urges, we cannot avoid such questions. "Man's search at midlife," says Peter Chew, "is ultimately a spiritual one."[2] And much of the impetus behind that search is the idea of death, especially one's own death.[3]

For a religious man like Hezekiah, the death sentence seemed a cruel end to a life that God had only begun to use. His illness probably seemed manageable until Isaiah's blunt words: "Put your house in order, because you are going to die; you will not recover" (Isa. 38:1). That is like a doctor's verdict following a person's annual checkup: "We've discovered an inoperable cancer. You have about six months to close out your business affairs and make your funeral plans." That is unwelcome news to any person who loves life and has expectations for several more years of it.

Even the precautions we take against the day of death include no thought of death's imminence. We provide a home for the family and invest in insurance. We take regular medical exams, save for the children's education, prepay our burial expenses, and write our wills. All these things we do wisely but with a sense of detachment as though we were handling plans for someone else. Death is hardly on our agenda.

What did the threat of death mean to Hezekiah? At the age of forty, a successful ruler in Israel, he felt the unfairness of death's visit. Life was to be cut short, like a shepherd's collapsing tent or a weaver's unfinished task (Isa. 38:12). Surely what Paul called the sting of death (1 Cor. 15:56) must include the fear of leaving behind an unfinished work. Hezekiah felt that Judah needed his leadership both politically and morally. Apparently he had no ready successor since Manasseh was born three years later. He must have wondered who would carry on his work. Fortunately, he would never see how wretchedly Manasseh performed as king!

Death cuts a gash in a family like a tornado's devastating march through a forest or a town. Our sense of mortality is heightened by the death of friends and family members. We come to see death as the great democrat that levels all persons and ends all hopes and dreams. Perchance this fact about life—the certainty of death—will guide us, as it did Hezekiah, to cast ourselves upon the mercy of God.

Response to Crisis

Human methods of coping with the stress of mid-life "range from martinis to meditation" and appear limited only by one's imagination.[4]

One frequent response is to defy the facts of life rather than to face them rationally. This reaction takes various forms.

1. Persons may turn to illicit sexual relationships. Through sexual binges a man seeks to assert his masculinity and prove his libido is still a reality. In so doing, he violates any covenant with the wife of his youth and demonstrates an immaturity that may destroy the marriage altogether. Professional men and women alike fall into this trap. Their number is legion.

2. Some individuals bury themselves in their work. The emptiness and anxieties they feel at mid-life will, they hope, be overcome by an extra devotion to their vocational interests. Work also seems a way to ensure economic security. A number of persons become workaholics. They thrive on activities associated with the business, for it fills a void in their lives. The stress accompanying a person's labors may give rise to cardiac distress, ulcers, and other health problems.

3. Mid-life crises lead often to career or job changes. People who have suffered burnout or loss of zest in their present positions hope for an exciting new life elsewhere. Discontent with self and one's job seem to be bedfellows. Recently, I counseled with a person who is somewhat weary of his work and is leaning toward a career change. This change would require a move to another state, the interruption of his wife's career, and the disruption of his children's education. All these challenges can be handled by this close-knit family but not without considerable strain.

Some individuals still dream, as they did in adolescence, of an ideal vocation, residential dwelling, marriage, and popular acclaim. Mid-life requires a reassessment of these dreams. Long ago, the Roman poet Horace noted the folly of running to new places to escape problems that are locked up within a person's own heart. You resolve issues where you are.

4. Mid-life brings attempts to conceal the aging process. To cover up

the signs of age, Americans annually spend millions on clothes, cosmetics, sport cars, fad diets, and plastic surgery. Someone has remarked that "when old peacocks begin to fade, they put on their brightest colors." Human vanity is quite costly. To accept our mortality is more realistic than to defy the facts of life. George Bernard Shaw used to amuse people by contending that he would never die. But George Bernard Shaw now is no longer here to make that boast!

5. Mid-life crises find some people ditching responsibility rather than facing it creatively. One favorite device is to shift responsibility to God. After all, He made us, gave us the appetites we seek to satisfy, and built us for obsolescence rather than perpetual youth. Initially, Hezekiah felt that his distress was heaven-sent. "He has spoken to me, and he himself has done this" (Isa. 38:15). Some persons search for God's help amid their difficulties. Others expect no such assistance since they ascribe painful circumstances to divine injustice.

Another way of ditching responsibility is that of *facing the wall* (Isa. 38:2), capitulating to moods of depression and defeat. To Hezekiah's credit, he turned his face to the wall to pray, not to yield to the crisis. Some adults fall for the old myths associated with mid-life, most of them related to the aging process. Without question, the middle years bring changes and constitute something of a transition period. But life ahead has promise, we are still capable of learning, we are able to solve problems and manage changes, we retain our powers of recall, and generally we have treasured friendships. This is no time to throw in the towel.

Take, for example, the old notion that adults learn little and retain even less. Educators have long since exploded that myth. Adult minds can fossilize or resemble blighted trees that die from the top, but only because reading, thinking, and seeking new truths have ceased. Learning is a lifelong pursuit.

In contrast to the above responses, religious faith presents a positive way of meeting mid-life crises. The critical middle years challenge us to draw on divine resources for the conduct of life. Hezekiah's response to crisis was to pray. Prayer for him was no last-ditch resort. Religious faith and prayer belonged to his life-style (2 Kings 18:3-7; Isa. 37:1-4,15-20;

38:2-3). Confronted by the prophet's death announcement, the troubled man quite naturally sought God's help.

Religious faith plays no such role in the experience of some adults. Gail Sheehy in *Passages* puts it bluntly: "Many people locked in early to a tight religious tradition find themselves struggling by midlife against absolutist positions that no longer correspond to their experience."[5] A religion expressed in rigid, legalistic terms or restricted to formal and ritualistic expressions may provide little help in testing times. Rather than a liberating force, it may be a burden. A strong personal faith in a living God will serve one well but not a secondhand faith.

Crisis has a way of testing religious faith. If hollow and formal, that faith may be set aside for some more promising savior. Faith that is solidly based upon a fatherly God will drive us to our knees before Him. From within that faith, we find answers to questions about life and its purpose, suffering and death, God and eternity.

Reliance on self fails us. Reliance on God opens a door for the second half of life.

Renewal of Life

Despite some acute problems during mid-life, for many of us this period has brought opportunities for growth, personal achievement, deepening of the marital bond, and enlarged faith in God. These renewing experiences have come not *despite* but *because* of the struggles and tests of the middle years. Renewal of life comes neither easily nor automatically to persons working their way through the transition. Most of us are indebted to family members for their patience and love, to the rational faculties that take life in hand, and especially to that inward strength given by the Spirit of God.

Hezekiah's experience reveals the part that genuine religion plays during a crisis. His faith gave him courage enough to question God's judgment (Isa. 38:3) and clarity of mind to see the growth potential of pain. "Surely it was for my benefit that I suffered such anguish" (38:17). There is no evidence that any idea of repudiating God or his faith ever crossed his mind. It was "a time not to lose religion but to use it" as my father once advised me while plowing in a stump-filled piece of land.

Hezekiah's postcrisis meditation reveals his acute distress before the cloud was lifted (38:9-14). His anguished cry, "I am troubled; O Lord, come to my aid!" brought a great relief. Out of it all emerged several positive results.

1. Hezekiah realized that we live because of the goodness of God. Life and all it involves is a gift from Him. "I have heard your prayer and seen your tears; I will add fifteen years to your life" (v. 5). A brush with death makes thinking persons reevaluate their lives. This man had heard what C. S. Lewis called God's megaphone—pain—and he had gotten the message. He came through the crucible with renewed faith and a firmer grip on God (38:15-17).

2. Hezekiah discovered afresh the mercy and forgiving love of God. "In your love you kept me/from the pit of destruction;/you have put all my sins/behind your back" (38:17). Forgiveness and mercy are needed at every stage of life. They keep us fit for fellowship with God and with persons about us (1 John 1:7).

3. Hezekiah's bout with death gave him a deepened sense of life's meaning and value, as well as its fragility (38:12). Reflective persons ponder their destiny, wonder about death, and seek those resources needed for the rest of their journey. They elect not to drown out these concerns with alcohol, drugs, illicit sex, or other obsessions.

The Bible teaches us to face the future prayerfully. "Teach us to number our days aright,/that we may gain a heart of wisdom" (Psa. 90:12). How much time do we have left on the clock of life? Should we not come to terms with the fact of death, especially our own? Mid-life is a good time for those considerations. It was for Don Witt. At mid-life this man received the death sentence from an examining physician. "You have leukemia of the worst sort. You have only a short while to live." A chemist employed by the state of Tennessee, Don was a devout Christian whose faith showed itself in that crisis. Said he, "I had always tried to live so that when the moment of death arrived, I would be ready for it. But I was so stunned by this news that initially I felt nothing." Miraculously, God gave Don an extension of life as He did Hezekiah. The cancer went into remission. In 1986, when we talked, Don had lived three-and-one-half years beyond the doctor's verdict. This man maintains a full-time job, directs an adult choir, teaches a Sunday School class, and plays a violin. He is a joyful soul who values each day as a special gift from God.

4. Hezekiah dedicated his life anew to God. Suffering and deliverance left him humble in spirit (38:15) and quick to praise the One who had lifted his sentence. Sheol, the shadowy realm of the dead, would have to wait to receive him (38:18-19a). Christians have a blessed hope that Hezekiah never knew. He faced death with courage but lacked the assurance of life beyond that Jesus provides. Life for us is no collapsible tent but a house not made with hands, eternal in the heavens (2 Cor. 5:1). For Jesus Christ, Lord and Savior, "has destroyed death and has brought life and immortality to light through the gospel" (2 Tim. 1:10).

An eternal hope energizes our present lives. We live daily under the hope of eternity. The life we offer up to God is really one He gave to us and renewed for us. It is kept alive by prayer and fellowship with the Eternal.

5

The Model Prayer
Matthew 6: 9-15

The Model Prayer is "the purest expression of the mind of Jesus. It crystallizes his thoughts. It conveys the atmosphere of his childlike trust in the Father. It gives proof of the transparent clearness and peace of his soul."[1]

In giving this Model Prayer, Jesus was responding to His disciples who wanted help with their praying (Luke 11:1). He was also protesting against long-winded prayers and hypocritical displays (Matt. 6:5-8). Praying, like other aspects of religious worship, He declared, must be simple, sincere, and from the heart. Is it not strange that we have taken the model intended to discourage "vain repetitions" and used it with tiresome repetition? This prayer can surely be recited sincerely, but Jesus' intention was to teach us the true dimension of prayer, not just to give us a prayer. He was encouraging the right kind of praying. "This is how you should pray" (Matt. 6:9). Here are the concerns that should flow through authentic prayer, the essential elements to include. Equally important, the Model Prayer focuses on the kind of spirit that should govern the one praying.

The Filial Spirit

We come to God as His children, not as outsiders. Jesus who enjoins us to pray "our Father" is the one who has made our relationship with God a reality. We are only prodigals, sinners saved by grace, claiming "no other right than that which is given us in the person of Jesus Christ."[2]

The idea of God as Father was not original with Jesus. Old Testament writers spoke of God's fatherly nature (Deut. 32:6; Isa. 63:16; 64:8; Mal.

1:6; 2:10; Ps. 103:13) as did Jewish rabbis prior to Christ. Generally, these references were to God as the Father of Israel. Jesus brought God close to each of us, revealing Him as personal, gracious in all His dealings toward us. His nature is love—indiscriminate and universal.

Jesus' use of the Aramaic word *Abba,* "Father" (Mark 14:36; see Gal. 4:6; Rom. 8:15-16) indicates His own intimate relationship to God. *Abba* belonged to the language of childhood and was equivalent to our word *daddy.* Aramaic usage probably lies back of the Greek word *pater* which occurs often on Jesus' lips. One thing is certain: Jesus everywhere spoke of God as Father. To understand the fatherly nature of God, we start with Jesus Himself. We do not begin with human fatherhood—even in its finest form—and by analogy arrive at a concept of God as Father. An earthly father might reveal God to us, but God is infinitely more than the best father we know (Matt. 7:7-11; Luke 11:13).

"Our Father in heaven" reminds us that He is high above us in holiness even though He is close beside us in love and mercy. "In heaven" refers not so much to geographical or spatial distance as it does to God's transcendence. God is far greater than our knowledge or experience of Him. Even Jesus confessed, "the Father is greater than I" (John 14:28). God is greater than any revelation of Himself. We hold Him in awe, for He occupies the immensity of the universe He created. He is perfect in power, knowledge, and love. Yet He is our Father who calls us to commune with Him. Our one hope is to look up and pray "our Father" and mean it.

To pray "our Father" means to acknowledge brothers and sisters in the Lord. Potentially, all persons belong to God by creation. But because of human sin and estrangement from Him, all relationships have been disrupted. God has taken steps to restore His fallen creation. Through the crucified Son, so Paul exulted, we become children of God by adoption. (Rom. 8:13-17,22-24). Receiving Jesus Christ brings birth into God's kingdom and all the rights that belong to His children (John 1:12).

Along with the rights and joys there come obligations and relationships. We belong to a family, and when we come before God we never come alone. This simply means that we are *one* with all others who share faith in Him. The company of the redeemed includes a wondrous variety in color, temperament, nationality, and gifts. Jesus Christ is the bond that holds all these together in one family under God. He creates a genuine brotherhood. This is far more than a fraternity built around selfish interests to accommodate a restricted group. In the family of God we learn to pray, "Our Father in heaven" (v. 9).

The Reverent Spirit

The Father God is ever near us, but let not familiarity breed contempt! "Hallowed be your name." "God's name," wrote Ernst Lohmeyer, "describes him in the totality, the uniqueness of his being and action."[3] That name is associated with ultimate power (Heb. 11:3), and He alone can use such power wisely. His name is linked with holiness. He is, as Isaiah kept saying, the Holy One. And He wants righteousness and justice to reign upon earth. This in a sense is what Jesus asks, that we implore God to make His holy will effective in the lives of people everywhere. A paraphrase of this petition might read, "Let your name as Father be the object of reverence and worship the world over."

What can we do to make God's name more hallowed or holy? Nothing! Nothing we say or do will add to His perfect goodness and holiness. God needs no one to defend His honor or protect His good name. When we attempt to shelter Him or protect Him, we show either ignorance or arrogance.

While we can add nothing to God's holiness, we can and must show reverence for His name. The reverential spirit forbids any attempts to limit God through misinterpretation or misuse of His name. Men have sometimes interpreted God in terms of power and force, thus seeking theological sanctions for their own coercive methods. Others have seen Him as the God of special interests, race, class, or economic and political systems. Those bound to rigid creedalism may see God as the great Lawgiver who holds people to strict obedience of discernible rules.

For all its faults, the "death of God" movement in the sixties challenged our glib use of God's name and our failure to reflect the Divine Presence in our living. We were judged guilty of spiritual forgery, taking the Name but denying the Reality. The loss of reverence for God may account in large measure for the irreverent spirit which permeates life today, the absence of sanctity for human life, and the junking of values once cherished.

Reverence is the soul of religion, and it grows out of a God consciousness. Reverence is fed by genuine worship (John 4:23-24; Jas. 4:8; Rev. 14:7), expressed in fidelity to God and a repudiation of idolatry (Deut. 13:17-18), and identity with Christ's spirit in our relationships with people. Thus do we show reverence for God's name.

The Submissive Spirit

Several years ago, Margaret Slattery wrote a book entitled *Thy Kingdom Come But Not Now*. Who wants God's kingdom, His sovereign rule with all its demands, here and now? A futuristic or eschatological kingdom is more to our liking! Walter Luthi suggested that about 90 percent of us pray, not "Thy kingdom come" but "My kingdom come."[4] Jesus, however, is unmistakably clear: Our prayer and our overwhelming concern must be for God's kingdom to come and His will to be done "on earth as it is in heaven" (v. 10).

Living in a society based on the rule of the people, we have little truck with kings and kingdoms. The little we know about kingdoms hardly applies to God's kingdom. For His is not geographical or spatial, national or racial. Nor it it statistical and visible. The kingdom of God refers to the realm of God wherein He rules absolutely. It is the realm of love, peace, righteousness, goodness, and mercy. Within that domain people obey Him faithfully and fully carry out the requirements of His holy will.

The Scriptures at times speak of a Kingdom that will come in the future when the powers of evil will be put down. For that we devoutly pray and wait in hope. But Jesus wants us to pray that people will increasingly submit themselves to God's rule right here on earth. The Kingdom is thus both present and future. While its consummation will come at Jesus' return, the Kingdom is here and now, and God's sovereign will is at work.

A saintly soul once declared that the kingdom of God is "humanity organized according to the will of God." But who does the organizing and who determines the content of the divine will? Only an incurable optimist willing to overlook the human capacity for evil expects human beings to create a perfect society on this planet. We do not "build the kingdom" or extend its controls. The Kingdom, as Jesus acknowledged, is God's gift to us (Luke 12:32). Doing His will (bringing life into line with His purpose) is possible only because of that grace which redeems us from sin and motivates us for righteousness.

What I have called the submissive spirit is more than a mere resignation to God's will. Praying "Thy kingdom come, Thy will be done" (KJV) means we are willing to be God's instrument to help bring that about. Jesus' example in the Garden of Gethsemane guides us. His prayer thrice offered, "Not my will, but thine, be done" (Luke 22:42, KJV) was far more than a stoic surrender to the inevitable. He became one with the work God was doing to reclaim a fallen creation. The submissive spirit for us is an active cooperation with God. In a true sense, it could be called the missionary spirit. We give feet to the prayer we pray.

The Dependent Spirit

Our dependence upon God makes prayer a necessity. That includes a petition concerning our physical needs. "Give us today our daily bread" (Matt. 6:11). A similar request occurs in Proverbs 30:8, "Give me neither poverty nor riches,/but give me only my daily bread." The concern for bread is as ancient as humankind.

The Bible sanctions a form of materialism, for it places value on the physical side of human existence. Jesus Himself teaches us that bread and the material aspects of life are continuing and lawful concerns. He who recognized that "Man does not live on bread alone" (Matt. 4:4) knew that persons do not live at all without bread. To make this petition refer to spiritual bread does an injustice to Jesus. He was thinking of physical food.

Can we expand the term *daily bread* to include our labor in producing goods, our health requirements, the soil underfoot, and the air overhead —all the things related to our physical existence? Some biblical interpreters think we can. Jesus, however, probably had the elemental need for bread in mind. He was thinking of persons who wondered each day how they would secure bread for the day. This prayer envisions no well-stocked larder, no luxury items, no extravagant indulgence of appetite. It tolerates no waste of precious food supplies.

Jesus' feeding of the multitudes, so John's Gospel indicates, was a sign of His messianic powers (John 6:26-40). It also showed His compassion for hungry people. God is interested in human welfare, concerned that all persons receive their daily bread. He has no delight in empty stomachs, or overstuffed ones for that matter. He does not will disease and poverty, nor is He honored by slums and substandard housing. He utterly condemns the calloused attitude that refuses to provide for the bodily needs of the poor (Jas. 2:15-16; 1 John 3:17-18).

Our daily bread is God's gift to us. But it comes from many sources and involves the toil of many persons. How can we overlook our indebtedness to all the people who make it possible for us to eat? Just as God's gift comes to us through others, even so must we pray that others may enjoy His gifts. "Give us today our daily bread" (v. 11).

There are certain implications growing out of this "us-our" petition. God owns the whole earth (Ps. 24:1). We are merely caretakers, and our lives are bound up together in our stewardship task. Gratitude to God saves us from pride in possessions. What we have received we must share with others (Isa. 58:7; Prov. 22:9). Christians keep the springs of compassion oiled with the grace of giving. World hunger is so massive today that the open heart must be matched by the open purse. How else can we honestly pray, "Give us today our daily bread"?

The Penitent Spirit

Our need for forgiveness is as universal as our need for bread. The readiness to forgive others is necessary for proper human relationships. Jesus put all this in one brief statement: "Forgive us our debts,/as we also have forgiven our debtors" (Matt. 6:12).

First of all, these words makes us face our sins. How could we deny them? We are born with sinning tendencies, surrounded by sinful people, and subject to recurring evil influences. "There is no difference, for all have sinned and fall short of the glory of God" (Rom. 3:23). Sin is alienation from God, but sin cannot provide ultimate escape from Him. For that reason we cry out, "Forgive us."

The Model Prayer in *Matthew* uses the term *debts* (*opheilēmata*) for sin. Luke's version has the term *sins* (*hamartias*). Jesus' brief commentary on sin and forgiveness (Matt. 6:14-15) employs the word *trespasses* (KJV) (*paraptōmata*). What are we to make of these variations? *Debts*—originally an economic term meaning actual, legal debts—here designates our moral and spiritual debts to God. We owe it to God to be obedient. Sin is the failure or unwillingness to discharge our obligations to Him. Luke wrote to a Gentile readership devoid of the religious understanding of ethical debt. He used the common Greek word *hamartia,* sin, to specify acts of transgression or wrongs done to other persons. *Trespasses* refers to unlawful or immoral acts against the person or property of another. It includes lapses or deviations from truth and uprightness.

All the above terms add up to a description of our moral failures, imperfections, and misdeeds against God and others. In the Model Prayer, Jesus did not indicate what brings us to a sense of guilt for sin. Elsewhere He noted that the Holy Spirit works in the heart to produce conviction for sin (John 16:8-11). As a result we pray, "Father, forgive us."

The one thing greater than our sinfulness is the love and tender mercy of a forgiving Father. His disposition to forgive hardly means that He overlooks the seriousness of wrongdoing. God forgives us on the basis of the crucified Christ. In some way the death of Christ in our behalf satisfies the holiness of a righteous God even as it discloses the love of God for us. Forgiveness is God's act of blotting out our sins and bringing us into right relationship with Himself.

A right relationship with God makes possible, even imperative, right relationships with persons. "As we also have forgiven our debtors"—the forgiven know how to forgive. As God's forgiveness removes the hindrances to fellowship with Him, so must we seek to remove barriers to fellowship between ourselves and others (Matt. 6:14-15; 18:15-35; Gal. 6:1; Eph. 4:31-32). Jesus plainly stated that persons incapable of offering forgiveness are incapable of receiving it. He hardly meant that we earn

God's forgiveness by forgiving others. But He recognized that "What blocks the flow of mercy or forgiveness *from* us blocks its flow *to* us."[6] The unforgiving spirit leads to the corrosion of the inner life and makes genuine worship and fellowship impossible (Matt. 5:23-24; Mark 11:25).

The Cautious Spirit

The Christian is a marked person, the special target of the evil one. Jesus, therefore, counseled caution: "Lead us not into temptation, but deliver us from the evil one" (Matt. 6:13). What did Jesus mean by temptation? In the biblical teaching, the word has two meanings: an inducement to moral evil (Gen. 3:1-6) and a trial or test (Jas. 1:12). In Jesus' thought, the reference was to moral evil.

Temptation comes from at least three sources.

(1) It comes *from within us,* from the region of our desires. Within us are hidden wells of desire (Jas. 1:14) that may lead to a host of sins (Mark 7:20-23). The weakness of the flesh gives evil enticement its chance, just as Achilles's heel invited Paris's fatal arrow. A wise man advises us to guard the inner life with vigilance since it is "the wellspring of life" (Prov. 4:23). Cautious persons will not allow evil to dwell in their minds, rove through their imagination, or dominate reason and emotion (see Josh. 7:20-21). Rather, they will "avoid every kind of evil" (1 Thess. 5:22) and use responsibly that freedom and power of choice that God gave them.

2. Temptation comes *from without.* The forgiven person lives in a society that is alienated from God and entrenched in evil. There is no easy way to insulate life against contacts with unregenerate people. We are thrust into situations fraught with moral peril and exposed to unholy speech and attitudes. We work alongside persons whose life-styles mock Christian values. With good reason we pray, "God, grant us help in the time of hard testing."

Temptation, so Martin Luther acknowledged, comes at us from the right and from the left. From the right come temptations associated with poverty, illness, marital troubles, bad fortunes, and slander. From the left come temptations related to wealth, success, health, and good fortune.[7] The stuff of which temptation is formed comes in a variety of circumstances. We pray earnestly for help against the slow infiltration of evil from our environment.

Temptation is connected with the work of Satan, the evil one. No child of God dare ignore the demonic element within human life. There is a powerful force at work in our world that is neither divine nor human. Satan is a master at disguise as Scripture observes (2 Cor. 11:14; 12:7; Rev. 12:9; 20:2). His most effective tactic is to make people deny that he exists.

Jesus never questioned the reality of Satan, His greatest adversary. Early in His ministry He encountered the evil one (Matt. 4:1-11). He saw Satan's involvement in all distortions of truth and the disruptions of life (Mark 4:15; Luke 13:16; 22:3,31; John 8:44). Paul counseled Christians to utilize the full armor of God because they were engaged in a powerful struggle with satanic powers (Eph. 6:11-12). Peter encouraged a spirit of self-control and alertness, since the devil is always on the prowl. "Resist him, standing firm in the faith" (1 Pet. 5:8-9).

Christians are caught between the victory of Christ's kingdom (Luke 10:18; Heb. 2:14-15) and the persistent onslaught of evil. We must have God's protection against sin and the moral perils we face each day. Thus we welcome the assuring word: "God is faithful; he will not let you be tempted beyond what you can bear. But when you are tempted, he will also provide a way out so that you can stand up under it" (1 Cor. 10:13). We know *some* of our limitations; God knows *all* of them.

The longer we continue in the Christian life, the more we come to loathe sin and fear its power. But the forgiveness that confers new life brings with it a strength against evil. We learn how to "watch and pray" (Matt. 26:41), "avoid every kind of evil" (1 Thess. 5:22), and find the way out of each temptation. We count especially upon Him who "knows how to rescue godly men from trials" (2 Pet. 2:9).

Years after Jesus gave the Model Prayer, there appeared a doxology for it (Matt. 6:13, KJV). One New Testament scholar thinks we owe this beautiful ending to the Syrian Church.[8] The purpose of the doxology likely was to make the prayer more suitable for congregational worship. In any case, the doxology provides a note of praise to the Father whose kingdom and power are secure and in whose will is our peace.

6

Between Believing and Nonbelieving
Mark 9: 14-29

Few biblical stories present as many interesting contrasts as the one
found in Mark 9:14-29. There we find agony and ecstasy, glory and
suffering, human weakness and divine power, faith and nonfaith, tragic
illness and healing goodness. Like so many biblical passages, this one
describes our condition and prescribes for it.

Faith and Failure

Individuals occasionally find themselves helpless in the face of dire
human need. Nine of Jesus' disciples had that kind of experience one day.
A distressed father brought his only son (Luke 9:38), described as demon
possessed and possibly an epileptic, and asked the disciples to heal the
lad. While it may seem strange to us that a person suffering the symp-
toms of epilepsy would be called demon possessed, it was not so in
biblical times. Indeed, first-century sources suggest that nearly all illnesses were thought to be caused by demons. Whether demon possessed
or epileptic, the severity of the boy's seizures indicated a serious illness
and justified the father's anxiety (see Mark 9:17-18).

Rather bluntly, the father stated the failure of Jesus' followers. "I
asked your disciples to drive out the spirit, but they could not" (v. 18).
That failure was a bit surprising in the light of earlier successes enjoyed
by these same men. Jesus had commissioned them to preach and heal and
had given them authority to drive out all demons (Luke 9:1-2). As a
result they "went from village to village, preaching the gospel and healing people everywhere (Luke 9:6). Their success was due to the power
Jesus gave them. It was not the result of any power inherent within

themselves (see also Luke 10:1-12,17). Perhaps they had forgotten this fact. At any rate, one by one they tried their hand to no avail.

When Jesus came on the scene, the disciples were busily engaged in a verbal exchange with the teachers of the law. Were the teachers (probably local rabbis) using the failure of the disciples in order to discredit Jesus? The world has often criticized Jesus and the Christian faith because of the failure of so-called Christians. Mark says the scribes were *arguing* with Jesus' disciples. The two groups ignored the human problem, burying it under an avalanche of heated words. Such in-house squabbling between religious parties amuses the world but never addresses its aching needs. Debating theological issues is a poor substitute for helping anxiety-laden, disease-ridden individuals.

How did the father of the boy feel as he stood with a restraining hand on the child while the religious experts conducted their word battle? Perhaps the crowd was beginning to jeer the disciples: "Where is your Master? Can't you do anything without Him?" The scorn of the crowd and the failure of the disciples conceivably shook the faith of the father and dashed his hopes to the ground. I agree with Reinhold Niebuhr:

> For every person who disavows religion because some ancient and unrevised dogma outrages his intelligence, several become irreligious because the social impotence of religion outrages their conscience. Religion never lacks moral fruits so long as it has any vitality.[1]

Jesus' appearance at the height of the crisis over the boy created quite a stir. "As soon as the people saw Jesus, they were overwhelmed with wonder and ran to meet him" (v. 15). They had surely seen Him before. Why, then, were they awed by His appearance? You will recall that He had just come from the mount of transfiguration. Possibly the people were impressed by His countenance, shining like that of Moses after his encounter with God on Sinai. Or their amazement could have been due to the opportuneness of His coming. He arrived at the right moment to meet a critical need the disciples had failed to handle.

Belief and Unbelief

Like a good physician, Jesus went straight to the father's problem. He listened to the man's analysis of the boy's illness and responded to the plea for help. Nothing in life is so eloquent as suffering love because it is so like divine love. Jesus' next step was to probe the man's soul, looking for evidence of faith. He had found little in His followers who, momentarily at least, had joined the "unbelieving generation." That failure on their part was enough to test the patience of their Teacher (Mark 9:19).

What kind of faith was Jesus expecting to find in the father? He used the man's desperate plea, "If you can do anything, take pity on us and help us," to test the degree of his faith (v. 21). It was a common practice with Jesus to evoke faith from persons looking for a miracle (Mark 1:40-42; 8:22-25; John 9:6,35-38). He wanted them to see the goodness of God and to build their lives upon Him. He never performed miracles to impress crowds or to establish Himself as a wonder worker. Persons healed, He hoped, would ascribe greatness to God.

Jesus turned the father's words back upon him. " 'If you can?' said Jesus. 'Everything is possible for one who believes.' " Jesus directed the distraught father to a fuller confidence in God. Faith, after all, reaches beyond oneself. It is a trustful reliance upon God who has power to act in our behalf. Faith is not some form of magic that can manipulate God, change His mind, or make Him grant our desires. Faith is the confidence that in every situation God will help us, either by altering the situation or enabling us to handle it.

The father's answer to Jesus is classic. "I do believe; help me overcome my unbelief!" (v. 24). He had some faith, and he prayed for more. In effect the father pleaded, "My boy needs healing. Do not deny him mercy because I lack a mature faith. Do not penalize him for my weakness of faith." An embryonic faith, though small as a mustard seed, catches the eye of God. It is strong enough to tackle all kinds of problems, for it views these from the perspective of God's matchless power (Matt. 17:20).

Some of us, like that father, know the tension between believing and not believing. Doubt and uncertainty invade the mind. Even mature people who have solid anchorage in the faith acknowledge this experience. Especially, those young and immature in the Christian life may be troubled by doubts.

A university student, suddenly thrust into a world of new ideas that challenged his unexamined beliefs, called his pastor in deep distress. "Some of these professors," he exclaimed, "don't believe in the virgin birth." His pastor abruptly replied, "Son, there are some days when I don't even believe in God!" That answer may puzzle us. Aren't pastors men of God who are absolutely certain that He is real and that life's perplexing problems have simple solutions?

Honesty leads us to confess, as do the saints of God through the ages, that sometimes God seems hidden from us, that harsh realities like suffering and evil baffle our best thinking. I find it comforting that God's people have repeatedly wrestled with problems of belief and unbelief. They never surrender their faith in Him, but they raise questions about His absence, His silences and what seems to be His rejection of them (Job 13:24; Ps. 10:1; 42:5-11; 44:9-26; 88:14; Jer. 12:1-4; Hab. 1:2-4; 2:1).

God is never embarrassed or threatened by any questions that we throw to Him. Chronic doubting can, of course, lead to a dead end. But God loves an honest interrogation mark in the mind of a sincere person. Indeed the Spirit of God excites our curiosity and guides inquiring minds into truth (John 14:16-17,26). An individual who never raises questions never knows the joy of discovery. "Help my unbelief" can be the prayer of one who stands on the threshold of new adventures in learning and growth.

Faith and Healing

Jesus' encounter with the father and his son brought both hope and healing. This incident highlights the role of faith in healing, but the focus rests upon the Healer. Should not all healing be seen as the gift of God regardless of how it comes? This is the point made by George Buttrick, even though he emphasized the place of prayer and faith in the healing process.[2] Jesus wasted no time in calling forth divine energies beyond human power to measure or comprehend. In so doing, He completely reversed a hopeless situation. Both the disciples and the crowd, viewing the miracle of healing, "were all amazed at the greatness of God" (Luke

9:43). Human effort devoid of divine power had failed. Jesus brought to the situation human compassion coupled with the power of God and a miracle took place.

> When Jesus comes the tempter's pow'r is broken;
> When Jesus comes the tears are wiped away.
> He takes the gloom and fills the life with glory,
> For all is changed when Jesus comes to stay.[3]

True faith looks to One who is the Lord of life. He is greater than all demons (real or imaginary), greater than all the destructive forces that prey upon life. The synoptic accounts of this incident make that clear. Satan is no match for Jesus Christ. He vented his hostility against the afflicted boy to such a degree that the people said, " 'He's dead.' But Jesus took him by the hand, lifted him to his feet, and he stood up" (vv. 26-27). Jesus' act disclosed a tremendous truth: Satan has been dethroned! Death has been challenged! Life has been affirmed!

The episode in Mark 9 forms the backdrop for Jesus' announcement of His coming death (9:30-32; see Luke 9:43-44). The crowning blow to the kingdom of evil and the one hope for our salvation came in the death of our Lord on the cross. It was there that the Son of woman lifted His bloody heel to crush the ugly head of the serpent (Gen. 3:15). Jesus' oneness with us in the struggle against temptation and sin came to a climax in His death. He was made perfect through suffering (Heb. 2:10,-14-18). He tasted death for us all. We believe that He thereby defeated the devil and ensured our life forevermore.

Faith and Prayer

Faith-weakness is a common malady. The remarkable thing is God's use of us anyway. Jesus' response to the father of the boy He healed indicates that God never waits until faith is fully mature before He acts in our behalf. Mustard-seed faith gets answers from Him. God understands our natures. We are called upon to present living sacrifices (Rom. 12:1), not perfect ones. God places the treasures of the gospel in common earthen vessels (2 Cor. 4:7). To use a rustic expression: He must often cut wood with a dull ax that has a crooked handle.

Even so, we are called to a lifetime of growth. No Christian should remain in the spiritual nursery, content with a beginner's faith and prayer. Growth is imperative because of the crucial role faith and prayer play in Christian worship and living. Prayer is the central act of faith, for it is faith in exercise.[4] Does this seem to play into the hands of glib persons who say, "If you just have faith, your prayers will be answered?" Persons of faith do find ready access to God through Christ. But faith does not guarantee the answer we seek to the requests we make of God. We learn this as we mature in our prayer life. We learn it also from Jesus' Gethsemane experience and Paul's failure to get a "thorn" removed. What we call the Bible's prayer promises must be read carefully and interpreted wisely.

T. W. Manson wrote with great discernment: "Faith is not just believing in God and putting all our needs into his hands. . . . Faith is silent prayer; prayer is spoken faith."[5] Such a praying faith makes a powerful impact on persons. My childhood was directly influenced by such a person, the godly wife of a village physician. This woman directed the children's department of the Sunday School. Her specialty was Scripture memorization and prayer coupled with a love for boys and girls. Her radiant face, kindly ways, and personal concern for me were the human factors in my conversion experience. Her favorite hymn was: "More about Jesus would I know." I often wondered how Mrs. Ollie Wood could know any more about Jesus than she showed in her life!

Jesus took time to teach His disciples that faith is really an "unconditional receptiveness to the action of God."[6] We are never to set limits to God's power. The prayer of faith thus takes us right to the power source, God Himself. Puzzled over their failure at healing, the disciples asked Jesus, "Why could we not drive out the demon?" His answer went straight to the heart of their failure. "This kind can come out only by prayer" (v. 29). They had presumed upon their own powers. Had their former successes in exercising demons made them overconfident so that they failed to call upon God in this instance? To cast out demons in Christ's name through the power of heaven is one thing, but to attempt it in one's own strength is to forget the power source.

The words of Jesus, "only by prayer," challenge our dependence upon methodology, organization, and human skills. These have value only when the power of God moves through our lives as we use them. The neglect of genuine prayer diminishes our effectiveness and robs our ministry of joy. The Book of Acts clearly demonstrates that sustained prayer, marked by a living faith, is the way a church gets its work done. Through sustained communion with God, the individual discovers the Power for combating evil and performing good.

Prayer and faith are bound together. They develop through use, not mere discussions. The best preparation for prayer is praying, and praying leads us into deeper faith.

7

Gratitude: Response to Grace
Luke 17: 11-19

In his Gifford lectures, John Baillie had a chapter on "Grace and Gratitude." According to him, "gratitude is not only the dominant note in Christian piety but equally the dominant motive of Christian action in the world. Such gratitude is for the grace that has been shown us by God."[1]

Our earliest lessons in gratitude may have been learned in a Christian home where prayers of thanksgiving were offered at mealtimes. This was my experience. My father was a man of simple faith. From earliest childhood, I learned from him that life moved between the poles of work and worship. Family meals always began with prayer. There was no rhetoric about Father's praying, only a brief word of gratitude for the food upon the table. But that plain ritual established in my young mind the importance of the grateful spirit.

Gratitude as a response to divine grace—and the contrasting spirit of ingratitude—appears in Luke's story about Jesus and ten lepers.

A Fitting Response

Gratitude is a fitting response to God's graciousness to us, His undeserving creatures. We share Jesus' disappointment that out of the ten persons He healed, only one returned to thank God for the gift of new life. Luke, the humanitarian, noted that this man was a Samaritan. We assume that the others were Jews.

Jews and Samaritans generally avoided one another (John 4:9). The ten lepers, however, formed a little community. They shared in a common misery and were bound together by suffering and isolation (Lev.

13:45-46). Crises, troubles, and dangers may weld diverse groups into a oneness for survival. During World War II, black and white soldiers from the United States fought side by side against a common enemy. This occurred before the armed forces were integrated by law. "We learn from pain, such is our stubbornness, truths we refused to learn from joy."[2]

Lepers were required by law to keep their distance from the rest of society. They were cut off from family, synagogue, and Temple. Healthy persons developed both fear and callousness toward these unfortunate wretches.

We can ill afford a sharp criticism of the polite society of Jesus' day. We also find ways to insulate our comfortable souls against undesirables. We restrict them to ghettoes and prisons, finding consolation in the view that such types will always exist or that they are responsible for their condition.

Jesus' quick compassion in the face of human need stands in sharp contrast to human callousness. On one occasion, He defied the Levitical law, reached out to touch a leper, and healed him (Mark 1:40-42). He had a way of identifying with suffering persons. To the ten who cried out for pity He simply said, "Go, show yourselves to the priests" (v. 14). The priestly certification of wholeness would liberate them and allow them to reenter society. "And as they went, they were cleansed." They received that miracle from God for which every leper hoped. Rotting flesh became vibrant with health, and sagging spirits revived at the wonder of healing.

One man, sensing that the gift of healing had come from God, turned back, "praising God in a loud voice. He threw himself at Jesus' feet and thanked him—and he was a Samaritan" (vv. 15-16). A double stigma had worked on this man's life. He was both a leper and a Samaritan. Did pain and ostracism produce in this outcast a sensitivity not found in the nine who were also recipients of mercy? His grateful response to divine grace marked him as a person worthy of emulation.

If gratitude is the proper response to God's goodness, why did the nine not also return to give thanks to God? Ray Summers surmised that these men were all Jews. Possibly they accepted healing as their due. They certainly were quick to obey the law which required a priestly examination before they rejoined family and friends in normal living.[3] Obedience to law came before gratitude for grace! Once on the way, the men did not find it convenient or expedient to lose time by turning back. These symbolize a host of ingrates who put expediency above everything else.

Did the nine feel that expressions of gratitude were unimportant? Multitudes of people in this age seem to hold that view. They are forever receiving but seldom acknowledge the Source of life's benefits. Ingratitude and forgotten kindness cut more sharply than a knife. An Old Testament story underscores this fact. Joseph, in prison for a false charge, performed a kindness to a fellow prisoner. That man was Pharaoh's butler, soon to be released. Joseph asked the butler to speak a word on his behalf to Pharaoh. But the official went two years with no thought of Joseph who continued to languish in prison (Gen. 40). Grateful remembrances are a fitting response to kindly deeds.

Procrastination accounts for many lapses in gratitude. Perhaps the nine men thought they would see the healer later and show Him their appreciation. But there is no record that they ever did. Some of our most painful memories revolve around expressions of love and gratitude we neglected to make. Thomas Carlyle, the notable Scotchman, wrote of his mother: "Oh, that I might have her back again to tell her with what love and veneration I ever regarded her as the most beautiful of all mortals." Feelings of gratitude should never be suppressed or their expression postponed. Someone has well said that "a flower in the hand is worth more than two on the grave."

A Spontaneous Response

Gratitude is a distinctive mood of the Christian life, a prominent element in worship and prayer. It is an ethical quality characteristic of reflective believers. Thoughtful persons are also thankful persons.

In thanksgiving, individuals show an awareness of their debt to God and to others. Gratitude acknowledges our sense of dependence. The apostle Paul regularly declared his personal appreciation for people who shared his ministry and met his needs. Consistently, Paul urged his readers to give thanks to God even as he himself did. Thanksgiving, he declared, is one of the basic forms of prayer (1 Tim. 2:1). His letters abound in allusions and admonitions concerning gratitude (Rom. 1:8; 1 Cor. 1:4; Eph. 1:16; 6:18; Phil. 1:3; Col. 1:3,11; 1 Thess. 1:2; 2 Thess. 1:3; 1 Tim. 1:12). Giving thanks amid all circumstances, good or bad, is "God's will for you in Christ Jesus" (1 Thess. 5:18).

Gratitude is an obligation, but it is far more than that. It is a spontaneous response to a grace freely given. The Samaritan's desire to voice gratitude to his benefactor took precedence over the demands of ceremonial religion. Jesus' gift of healing touched off emotional vibrations in the leper's soul. Priestly certification, the man felt, could come later.

Gratitude here took the form of exuberant praise. There is a naturalness and freedom about the leper's action. The one constraint was his own throbbing desire to express the deep feeling of his soul. Falling prostrate at Jesus' feet was his way of acclaiming the Master. The spontaneity and joy marking his behavior reminds one of the woman's anointing of Jesus. With her heart overflowing in love and gratitude for her Lord, she broke the narrow-necked bottle and lavishly poured the expensive liquid on Jesus' head (Mark 14:3-9).

Genuine, spontaneous praise electrifies worship and startles the sophisticated who value order, control, and stated forms. I am afraid the Samaritan would disturb some staid congregations with their predictable styles of worship. He might be too Pentecostal or charismatic for our easygoing churches. Our carefully edited and time-bound worship, marked by delicate artistry and cracker-dust sermons, allows no place for spontaneous outbursts. Those who want to enjoy their religion must be careful not to do it at church!

Gratitude need not be boisterous, but it must be evident and frequently expressed. Its opposite, ingratitude, damages the individual. Ingratitude is a base sin rooted in a person's egotistical nature. Karl Barth called it our most common and reprehensible sin. It produces a whole brood of evils.

Ingratitude intensifies selfishness, ignores our creaturely dependence on God, and causes persons to manipulate others for selfish gain. Ungrateful people become like the Dead Sea, forever receiving and never giving. The fountains of goodness and kindness run dry in their lives. They breed pessimism and thrive on negativism.

Ingrates can be found in all classes and social groups though the affluent are especially vulnerable. One of the crowning sins of the Roman world, so Paul charged, was the spirit of ingratitude. Members of the ruling society "neither glorified him as God nor gave thanks to him" (Rom. 1:21). Worldly wealth and wisdom made them feel self-sufficient and unmindful of God. Out of that arrogant egotism arose a multitude of vices (Rom. 1:22-32).

Grateful people transform life about them. They find ways to honor the Lord for all His benefits (Ps. 116:12-13). Their lives reflect sunshine and goodness, telling the world of His works "with songs of joy" (Ps. 107:22).

A Continuing Response

Gratitude is a continuing response to a continuing grace. Divine mercies are new each morning (Lam. 3:22-23) so that we never face the day's struggle with depleted energies. Unfailing love calls for unfailing thanksgiving (Ps. 107:31). Sporadic acts or an annual Thanksgiving Day are inadequate responses to God's consistent goodness toward us.

In a good marriage, love and appreciation is the language used by devoted mates. Who wants to be like the man who said, "When we got married, I told her I loved her. That still holds good. When it doesn't, I'll let her know." A wife deserves more than that. A marriage survives and thrives when mates frequently express mutual love and appreciation. Similarly, the Christian life is enriched when we regularly express gratitude to God. We thank Him for all the good things that come through Jesus (Rom. 8:32). The steady flow of divine mercies into our lives merits a continuous thanksgiving.

What about people whose response to God's gracious gifts is silence? Jesus' reaction to the ingratitude of the nine healed lepers suggests God's own view of thanklessness. "Were not all ten cleansed? Where are the other nine? Was no one found to return and give praise to God except this foreigner?" (v. 17).

The silent nine typify the ungrateful souls in every generation. They represent thankless persons *outside* the church. Even nonreligious people prefer stable, crime-free communities. They are the beneficiaries of a culture that has been influenced by Christianity. Religious persons stand for law and order. They believe in honesty and justice and demonstrate compassion and neighborliness. The Christian faith has given birth to schools, hospitals, orphanages, and other humane institutions. It has influenced business, education, and government. The church often ministers to outsiders in their times of crisis. For all these reasons, nonbelievers should be grateful. They receive many benefits from living in a community influenced by godly people.

Ingratitude often is found *within* the church membership. Members ask God for mercy but forget to thank Him for all the blessings received. They pray for the removal of thorns and for solutions to critical problems. Weekly prayer meetings sometimes sound like sick call! Seldom do we spend time praising God for all the help He has given us, for lives rescued from sin, for homes restored, and for special grace extended us. Our prayers of petition far outnumber our prayers of thanksgiving. Undoubtedly the absence of thankfulness accounts for the lack of joy among God's people. Gratitude and joy are linked in Scripture and in the lives of devoted Christians.

Thoughtful people acknowledge their indebtedness to God and to persons through whom divine love and benevolence come. There is a long list of individuals who have touched our lives and made them better. Gratitude begins at home. "Honor your father and your mother," says an ancient commandment (Deut. 5:16) which has never been revoked. Obedience to that law means respect and appreciation for parents. Within the family circle, the spirit of thanksgiving challenges self-centeredness. Love and tender expressions of appreciation by parents provide a model for children and are far more effective than lectures on being grateful.

Our debt of gratitude extends to teachers, pastors, and close friends who have helped shape our thoughts and mold our ideals. Significant persons in our lives have provided counsel, financial assistance, and encouragement when most needed. Many of them are no longer living, but we thank God upon every remembrance of them.

The prayer of thanksgiving takes in all the things God provides for daily living. A hymn writer has urged: "Count your many blessings, name them one by one, and it will surprise you what the Lord hath done."

We learn, as Paul did, that God's treasures are inexhaustible, that He is "able to do immeasurably more than we ask or imagine" (Eph. 3:20).

God's rich grace is undeserved. Gratitude accordingly is a natural expression of one whose faith has claimed that grace. "Your faith has made you well," Jesus said to the thankful Samaritan (v. 19). To be made well meant rescue from impending destruction or some grave danger (see Matt. 9:21-22; Mark 5:23,28-34; 10:52; Luke 8:36,48,50; 18:42). God had established a beachhead in the Samaritan's heart. He was rescued from a physical illness, but, even more, his life was changed and set upon a new course.

Christian gratitude, like contentment, never depends on external circumstances. It is a response to God's love and strengthening grace which undergird life during all seasons.

To the world's amazement, Christians maintain their hopes and show forth the praises of God even in the worst of times. Martin Rinkhart (AD 1586-1649) illustrated that phenomenon. He ministered in Eilburg, Germany, during the Thirty Years War. The walled city was a refuge for fugitives. Overcrowded and unsanitary, the city bred famine, disease, and death. During the great pestilence of 1637, Rinkhart was the only pastor available. He had responsibility for burying thousands of victims, often forty or fifty persons a day. He lost his own wife during this period. The faith that sustained this godly man found expression in a hymn written by him one year earlier (1636). Strangely, the title of that hymn (still in wide use today) is "Now Thank We All Our God." One stanza is enough to disclose Rinkhart's indomitable spirit:

> Now thank we all our God
> With heart and hands and voices,
> Who wondrous things hath done,

In whom his world rejoices;
Who, from our mother's arms,
Hath blessed us on our way
With countless gifts of love,
And still is ours today.

8

Getting Through to God
Luke 18: 9-14

Have you ever had extensive X rays of your internal organs? That is no experience to covet. But it is most revealing when the pictures appear on a screen before your eyes. Your stomach, for instance, looms before you like a large pear or some sort of jug. From the moment you don the ill-fitting gown until the technician releases you, you feel exposed and undignified—but well photographed. A skilled reader finds those X rays a genuine aid to understanding your physical condition.

In Jesus' parable of the Pharisee and the publican, He revealed the inner nature of two men before God. God alone knows us fully. We cannot wholly know another person and possibly never completely know ourselves. We do, however, reveal ourselves through the words we speak, the attitudes we display, the conduct we show, and the prayers we pray. That is the point Jesus made in the parable. Our private prayers, if heard by a discerning person, would give us away. Public prayers may also disclose the depth or shallowness of our spiritual lives.

When Jesus wished to reveal the contrasted character of the Pharisee and the tax collector, He showed them both at prayer. The scene occurred in the Herodian Temple at Jerusalem where the official hours of prayer were 9:00 AM and 3:00 PM "Two men went up to the temple to pray" (v. 10). They went up in Jesus' day; they still may be found—these contrasting types—in our places of worship today. Jesus must have shocked His hearers by this story. He made the good man a villain and the bad man a hero! How could the Pharisee, with so many good deeds to his credit, be so odious to God? How could the tax collector, with such a dismal record, find his way into God's favor?

The unfolding of this parable's truth indicates the perils that attend the path of religious profession and practice. It also points up the spirit that must characterize saint and sinner alike.

A Phony Piety

George Foot Moore's classic work on Judaism pays tribute to the merits of historic Jewish religion and discourages superficial criticism of this noble faith. Jesus' negative view of the Pharisee applied not so much to adherents of Judaism as it did to a particular religious mentality that caused persons to exalt themselves above others. An effective religion hardly avoids those forms utilized by the Pharisee. It does avoid this Pharisee's spirit.

At this point, let us say a kind and fair word for the Pharisee lest we prove guilty of "outphariseeing" him. Look at some of his merits. He did go to church, attending worship with regularity. Also he spent some time at prayer, a practice neglected by multitudes of respectable church folks. He exercised self-discipline enough to engage in fasting, even going beyond the demands of his religion. "I fast twice a week," though the norm was once a year. He tithed carefully, giving one tenth of all he received (see Deut. 14:22-29; Matt. 23:23), a practice that many Christians find difficult to match. This man seemed to be a respectable person, living by the standards prescribed by his faith. He attended to the niceties of the moral code and faithfully obeyed the statutes of the Law.

Jesus, however, saw many faults in this man. These centered in his religion and surfaced in his praying. Defective prayer emerges from immature and self-centered religious faith. There is a type of religion which can come between a person and God. That may sound odd, but it was true of the Pharisee. It is equally true of the religiosity that becomes a substitute for true faith. The late J. H. F. Peile, nearly fourscore years ago, declared that people have been inoculated with a mild form of Christianity which renders them immune to the real thing![2]

Though Jesus did not list the false notes in the Pharisee's religion, his portrait of the man disclosed at least three distinct fallacies.

1. The Pharisee counted too heavily upon the value of religious observances. His dependence upon ritual religion was evident from his Temple

prayer. Jesus, like Israel's great prophets, castigated any religion strong on ceremony and form but heartless toward persons. Churchgoing and fidelity to worship forms are a part of genuine faith. But these must contribute to ethical living and the transformation of human relationships. Worship, preaching, and prayer should charge our spiritual batteries and motivate us for actions true to Christ's spirit. When these are related to modern need, touching people where they live, life is infused with meaning and lifted above superficialities.

Jesus challenged the smugness and complacency of individuals "who were confident of their own righteousness" (v. 9). Apparently, such persons viewed righteousness as conformity to external rites and rules.

Jesus resisted the legalistic mentality that measured righteousness in terms of specific ritual or moral acts. He challenged the narrowness of mind that determined orthodoxy by one's adherence to stated beliefs, selected morals, and ritual worship performed in designated places. Jesus disallowed any creedalism that stifled an adventurous kingdom righteousness or aligned persons against their fellows. "I tell you," He declared, "that unless your righteousness surpasses that of the Pharisees and the teachers of the law, you will certainly not enter the kingdom of heaven" (Matt. 5:20). Justice, mercy, and faith are key elements within the kingdom of righteousness. They rank far above ritual acts such as fasting and tithing (Matt. 23:23-24).

2. The Pharisee's worship was wrecked by his pride. A spirit of pride and self-congratulation ruled and ruined his prayer. Jesus described the man's prayer as a monologue, not a dialogue with God. The Pharisee used God's name, but he prayed to himself! "The Pharisee stood up and prayed about himself; 'God, I thank you that I am not like all other men—robbers, evildoers, adulterers—or even like this tax collector' " (v. 11).

Prayer is a time for a reverent approach to God, a confession of one's sins, a grateful acknowledgment of God's gifts, and an earnest intercession for others. The Pharisee's mind was wandering, falling critically upon a fellow worshiper. He failed to realize that "in prayer we look up in aspiration or we look down in humility; we never look around in criticism or curiosity."[3] Is that why we close our eyes when we pray?

Worship, as the parable indicates, is vitiated by that pride which produces contempt for persons. Jesus knew that people with hatred and disdain for others can never worship effectively. In vain we approach the altar with gifts to honor the God whose image we despise in others. God hears no prayer that rises from a heart filled with hatred for individuals (Matt. 5:22-24; Mark 11:25). Nor can we sincerely call God "our Father" when we insultingly call our brother "fool" (Matt. 5:22).

Authentic praying forbids the unholy sport of judging others harshly. The proper attitude for Christians is that shown by Richard Baxter, the seventeenth-century Puritan saint. On observing the moral degradation of persons, Baxter would remark, "There, but for the grace of God, go I." For the Pharisee, the word *I* was central, but his inflated ego led him to look with condescension upon others. Freedom from the sins of adultery, extortion, and injustice certainly is commendable. That freedom, however, brings no right to sit in moral judgment upon others.

Somehow the Pharisee had missed the caution sounded by an ancient proverb: "Pride goes before destruction,/a haughty spirit before a fall. Better to be lowly in spirit and among the oppressed/than to share plunder with the proud" (Prov. 16:18-19).

3. The Pharisee lived with the mistaken notion that one can pile up merit before God. Meritorious conduct is great, but we weary of persons who are forever lauding their good deeds and fine achievements. True goodness and worthy conduct deserve recognition, but why not let God or other persons acclaim it?

Righteous actions flow naturally from the life that Christ has claimed. But they can never be stockpiled so as to put God in our debt. The Pharisee's piety, reflected in his tithes and fasts, brought God under no obligation to him. Many people, however, feel that they earn a good standing before God and a right to be rewarded for their good deeds and meritorious service. Like the elder brother, they feel that years of obedience and service deserve suitable reward (Luke 15:29). Thus when crises and calamities arise, they bitterly ask, "Why has God allowed this to happen to us?" Humanly speaking, people are always looking for their "well-deserved honors." Jesus counters this attitude by a reminder that faithful performance is nothing more than one's due to God (Luke 17:7-10).

The path of prayer must not be dogged by the old superstition that the rendering of our gifts and services obligates God to grant our requests. Rather we bring to the moment of prayer a sincere love for Him who first loved us. Divine grace, not our works or our merit, has saved us and now sustains us. Awareness of this should bring freedom and spontaneity to our praying.

A Perennial Pharisaism

The pharisee with his self-righteousness and scorn for others is always with us. He continues to intone his prayers, to be found often at church, and to expect God to reward him for being such a decent fellow. The modern pharisee comes in a variety of types.

1. There is the *intellectual* pharisee. Obviously, education and intelligence are noble assets. The command to love God with the whole mind (Matt. 22:37) gives sanction to institutions of learning and puts a premium upon the development of the intellect. A well-informed mind enhances opportunity for service and equips one for a worthy contribution to society. At the same time, a little learning may make a fool or produce a sense of pride and snobbishness. "Lord, I thank you that I am not crude and illiterate and without the advantages that belong to the educated."

A college diploma for some is a badge of sophistication. Possession of academic degrees may signal genuine learning. Education and social experience undeniably alter our relationships with our fellows. The advantages brought by education, however, need not feed our ego or produce a sense of pride. Too often our educational opportunity is provided by plain loving persons who lack formal training. "Education is a responsibility, a trust which we are charged to administer for the benefit of others. It is not an empty decoration to be worn with exultation."[4]

2. There are *social* pharisees. They have no higher ambition than to climb the social ladder, to be numbered with the socially elite, and to make the newspaper's society page. Then they can look out of their proud, empty minds at the inferior people beneath them.

Social pharisees have a false sense of values and may be devoid of authentic culture. Their tastes and life-styles frequently are marked by superficiality, and they make little contribution to the true well-being of their community. When we check their aspirations by the spirit of Jesus, they come up short. Unfortunately, the snobbish spirit invades some churches. A congregation dominated by class consciousness may be more like a social club than a church of the living Christ. Its members find the gospel terribly offensive. An elderly pastor of such a church counseled his ambitious young assistant, "To get along in this church, son, a man's preaching must avoid two subjects: politics and religion!" Such advice hardly fits the will of Him who makes no artificial distinctions between persons (Acts 10:34-34).

3. There are *racial* pharisees. No one would deny that the main racial groupings are different from each other. These differences are not defects. They only illustrate the rich variety within God's creation. Racial differences cannot be used to establish the superiority of one race and the inferiority of another. What some term superiority or inferiority is often due to accident of birth, environment, or educational and economic privilege.

The racial pharisee sometimes has distorted Scripture in the effort to ascribe superior-inferior categories to God's will for the human family. Is it not pathetic when Christians search the Bible to find sanctions for their prejudices and hatreds?

How does this kind of pharisee pray? "God, I thank you that I belong to the preferred race. I am glad that I am not a Jew, a Japanese, a Russian, a Black, or any other lesser breed."

4. There are *sectarian* Pharisees. These are the proud persons who claim superiority, if not sole genuineness, for their denomination or religious group. They stand for the faith once for all delivered to the saints but feel that God delivered it only to their address. Jesus, you remember, prayed for His followers that they might "all be one" (John 17:20). Within that prayer it is possible to maintain some differences of opinion. But we cannot depart from His spirit or refuse to love and respect one another.

Love of self more than love of truth drives a wedge between church groups. Gratitude for one's religious heritage never requires the disparagement of others. We certainly do not need to emulate the narrow-minded man who declared that even some of his own crowd would never make it to heaven!

A Line to God

A despised tax collector rather than a pious Pharisee received answer to his prayer. Jesus' compassion for tax collectors and harlots was well known (Matt. 9:10; 11:19; 21:31-32; Mark 2:14-17; Luke 15:1-2). But to make a tax collector the hero in a prayer parable must have amazed and angered some of His hearers. Tax collectors have never been as popular as Santa Claus, but in Jesus' day they were especially repugnant. What caused this excessive animosity?

Tax collectors were paid agents of the hated Roman government. Their association with Gentiles rendered them unclean ceremoniaily. Rabbinical students were forbidden to eat with them because they were "sinners." Local collectors were regarded as traitors to the nation as well as offenders against Jewish religion. In addition, many collectors resorted to extortionary practices. Zacchaeus, on his conversion, set about to make restitution of any wealth attained dishonestly (Luke 19:8). He admitted that he may have been a robber.

Despite all his shortcomings, the tax collector in Jesus' parable got through to God. From him we discover insight into the right approach to our Maker.

1. Consider the man's utter humility before God. His posture in prayer was identical with that of the Pharisee. Both *stood up,* the common Jewish posture in prayer. But they were poles apart in spirit. The tax collector felt even lower than the person described by the Pharisee. He was unwilling to lift up his eyes to heaven. The thought of a holy God made him deeply conscious of his own moral impurity. A similar awareness wrung from Isaiah the cry, "Woe to me! . . . I am ruined! For I am a man of unclean lips (Isa. 6:5). It led Paul to cry out despairingly, "What a wretched man I am! Who will rescue me from this body of death?" (Rom. 7:24).

Did the publican feel awkward and out of place in the Temple? He certainly kept his distance from other worshipers. His agonizing sense of guilt led him to beat repeatedly upon his breast—the expression of deepest contrition and sorrow (see Luke 23:48). While the Pharisee looked upon others as sinners, this man thought of himself alone as "the sinner." The word *sinner* (*hamartóloi*) ment one devoted to sin, pre-eminently sinful, stained with vices and evils. Humility of spirit like that man showed is not a form of self-hatred but an estimate of one's true nature when confronted by a holy God. Such a spirit should characterize all our prayers.

2. The tax collector showed a penitence of soul which pleases God (Ps. 51:17). Genuine prayer must always acknowledge our oneness with sinful humanity. We know our waywardness and our need for divine grace.

A penitent person is in a position to receive help. Broken in spirit, the tax collector tore his heart out of his breast and threw it down before God: "Here is my heart, fouled by evil, covered over with wickedness. Have mercy on me, O God. Cleanse my life and make me whole." This confessional approach to God leads to inner peace, joy, and satisfaction.

> Blessed are the poor in spirit,
> [those who know their spiritual poverty]
> for theirs is the kingdom of heaven.
> Blessed are those who mourn,
> [those who sorrow because of their sins]
> for they shall be comforted (Matt. 5:3-4).

Penitence must live with saints as well as sinners. This much we learn from Paul. For all his goodness and faithful ministry, Paul referred to himself as the worst of sinners (1 Tim. 1:15-16). Martin Luther, toward the end of his life, declared, "We are all beggars, that is true." Someone else has said:

> O break, O break, hard heart of mine,
> Thy weak self-love and guilty pride
> His Pilate and His Judas are:
> Jesus my Lord is Crucified.

3. The tax collector had a longing for God. Is not such a hunger built

into our nature? The God who made us in His own image created us for fellowship with Himself. Even our crude idolatries attest our spiritual nature. When we turn from God, we invariably resort to substitutes for Him. We are indeed incurably religious. But idols are a poor substitute for the true and living God, for only God can satisfy the hunger in our souls.

The tax collector, therefore, was on target in his supplication. He showed a kinship with the psalmist: "As the deer pants for streams of water,/so my soul thirsts for you, O God./My soul thirsts for God, for the living God" (Ps. 42:1-2). A person with that kind of spiritual appetite will not be turned away. "Blessed are those who hunger and thirst for righteousness,/for they shall be filled" (Matt. 5:6).

Despite a deep longing for God, fellowship with Him becomes possible only when the barrier of sin has been lifted (Isa. 59:1-2). We cannot handle that barrier, but God can. He responded to the tax collector's desperate plea. As Jeremias said, He is a God of the despairing and shows great mercy for those broken in spirit.[5] Did not Jesus say of the tax collector, "I tell you that this man, rather than the other, went home justified before God" (Luke 18:14)? This is the only place in the Gospels where the word translated "justified" has a Pauline sense. God forgave the man's sin, gave him a new nature and a new standing with Himself.

Two men went up to the Temple to pray. Both used the name *God*. With that, their similarity ends. One humbly confessed his sins; the other thanked God for his merits. One man's pride and self-sufficiency clouded his prayer; the other's sense of need and dependency led him to plead for mercy. Jesus knew that both men were guilty before God but that divine favor comes only to persons who share the penitent spirit. Is that not still true?

There is an old hymn which each of us should sing from the heart, for it declares a need we all know:

> Just as I am, without one plea,
> But that thy blood was shed for me,
> And that thou bidd'st me come to thee,
> O Lamb of God, I come! I come!

Just as I am, poor, wretched, blind;
Sight, riches, healing of the mind,
Yea, all I need in thee to find,
O Lamb of God, I come! I come!

Just as I am, thy love unknown
Has broken every barrier down;
Now to be thine, yea thine alone,
O Lamb of God, I come! I come!

Father, Forgive Them
Luke 23: 33-38

From the battlefields of the world, like lovely lilies scattered over a wasteland, come stories that reveal the greatness of the human spirit. The quality of a Christian heart is suggested by the story of an American soldier who was killed on Luzon in World War II. With some premonition of what might happen, he wrote his parents and stipulated what use should be made of his government insurance. The money, he said, should provide a scholarship for some Japanese student at an American college. His parents honored that request. A Japanese lad from Tokyo entered Lafayette College in Pennsylvania. He wrote: "I shall make the best possible use of this gift. I want to repay them as much as I can for the loss of their son."

The young American soldier had won the victory over hatred. His own death became the occasion for blessing an enemy. Where do people get the will for that kind of deed? Surely it comes from Jesus Himself. Jesus' first utterance from the cross—a cross set up by vicious, hate-filled persons—was a prayer for the forgiveness of the people who strung Him up like a common criminal. "Father, forgive them, for they do not know what they are doing" (v. 34).

Practicing the Teaching

Thomas Carlyle called Jesus' prayer for His enemies the sublimest words ever uttered by human lips.[1] More than that, the prayer was in line with His teachings about the treatment of one's enemies. Jesus never stood apart from the human situation, content to send out prescriptions for governing conduct. Rather, He demonstrated in His own life the things He asked of others. More than anyone who ever lived, He practiced what He preached.

To a generation comfortable with the Old Testament ethic, "an eye for an eye," Jesus' words about loving one's enemies sound unrealistic.

> Love your enemies, do good to those who hate you, bless those who curse you, pray for those who mistreat you. . . . Love your enemies, do good to them, and lend to them without expecting to get anything back. Then your reward will be great, and you will be sons of the Most High, because he is kind to the ungrateful and wicked (Luke 6:27-28,35).

Jesus' command that we love fellow Christians is sometimes difficult to obey, but the injunction to love enemies seems impractical and impossible. Men like Friedrich Nietszche have termed Jesus' teaching a philosophy for weaklings and have preferred the Mosaic code with its provision for retaliation. Jesus, however, canceled out the law of tooth and fang, replacing it with His gospel of love, forgiveness, and active goodwill (Matt. 5:38-42; see Rom. 12:17-21). From the cross, He demonstrated the ethic of love that He had taught.

The way Jesus handled bitter hostility directed at His person (Heb. 12:3) had a profound impact upon His followers. His prayer for His enemies found echo in the dying Stephen's words, "Lord, do not hold this sin against them" (Acts 7:60). The martyr's courage and love may have left its mark on the fanatical Pharisee Saul who later became God's apostle to the Gentiles. Despite the pain of the cross and cruel human rejection, Jesus' matchless expression of love achieved our redemption, so His followers believed.

> When they hurled insults at him, he did not retaliate; when he suffered, he made no threats. Instead, He entrusted himself to Him who judges justly. He himself bore our sins in his body on the tree, so that we might die to sins and live for righteousness; by his wounds you have been healed (1 Pet. 2:23-24).

Would Jesus have won our love and achieved our redemption had He answered force with force? He was not powerless, as He reminded Pilate. He needed only a gesture to bring a legion of angels to His defense (John

18:36; Matt. 26:53). But He refused coercive methods. Rather, His way of conquering evil and hate was by love's goodness. Evil, He knew, was a formidable force which must be rendered powerless. Jesus thus advocated no spineless, passive tolerance of evil. But He returned good for evil and conquered enmities by love, a force higher than hate.

Persons who would practice forgiving love—not just talk about it—must, like the Master, live in close touch with God. The gentle answer that turns away wrath (Prov. 15:1) rises out of a spirit under divine control. The love that conquers hate belongs only to persons who belong to Him.

Assessing Evil

The mystery of iniquity (2 Thess. 2:7) came into full view in the cross event. The men who arrested, tried, and killed Jesus were wicked to the core. No explanation or excuse for their treachery and foul play was contained in Jesus' prayer. Caiaphas, the priest, had a heart black as midnight and bitter as gall. Pilate was a politician given to expediency, a man marked by moral cowardice. The unthinking mob looked on without compassion as the Roman soldiers, calloused and accustomed to brutality, carried out the order to execute Jesus. Jesus' followers, lacking in courage, had fled from the scene of carnage.

Human nature revealed its capacity for evil the day Jesus died. But that evil neither originated nor ended at the cross. After twenty centuries, the ugly sins that caused persons to dispose of Jesus still find a home in our hearts. Some of life's tragic ills have been conquered by science and technology, but sin persists and must be dealt with in each generation. Sin cannot be educated out of the human race. Nor can it be removed by scientific methods or by cultural devices. How common are the sins that crucified Jesus—prejudice, a narrow religious and racial pride, barrenness of faith, hate, bitterness, jealousy, and fear. Who among us is absolutely innocent?

Behind specific sins such as those listed above is a *bad nature,* a self set against God, a life headed for destruction. The crucifixion of Jesus shows the utmost in human degradation, the limits to which evil will go in achieving its purposes. But the Christ of the cross is the one means by which human nature can be set right. Otherwise, "the soul who sins is the one who will die" (Ezek. 18:4), not merely a physical death but a spiritual death.

Jesus' prayer for his killers did not overlook their guilt or the fact that wicked persons come under God's judgment. God hates evil in every form and ultimately He will destroy it. But over against the background of eternal judgment stands the sure mercy of God. Blocking the road to hell is the cross and its appeal to repentance. And on that cross is one who loves even the worst of persons.

The man on that cross was totally devoid of hatred for people. He revealed to us a God who despises our sins even while He loves us. And God loves us all the time, not only after our repentance and acceptance of His way. "God demonstrates his own love for us in this: While we were still sinners, Christ died for us" (Rom. 5:8). Divine love does not overlook sinful human nature or its gross immoralities. The divine intention is to deal with the lostness and sheer helplessness of persons. Jesus' prayer showed His oneness with God's purpose to rescue a fallen humanity.

Recognizing Ignorance

Much of the evil in life, as John Claypool noted, is "rooted in blindness as well as in badness." Is that why Jesus prayed, "Father, forgive them, for they do not know what they are doing" (v. 34).? Some New Testament interpreters feel that this prayer was primarily for the Roman soldiers. These soldiers carried out the orders to execute Jesus, seeing Him only as an ordinary prisoner. At the moment of Jesus' intercession, they were gambling at the foot of the cross, His clothes being the prize. Their deed was insensitive and without concern but without malice. Jesus thus prayed for them that somehow they might come to know His true identity, that understanding might replace ignorance and lead to divine forgiveness.

Must Jesus' prayer be limited to the Roman soldiers? The words *forgive them* could include all Jesus' enemies, perhaps the whole mass of humanity for whom He died. Ignorance in the Bible often means more than the absence of factual information. Hosea attributed Israel's widespread immorality to the nation's ignorance of God (Hos. 4:1-6). Ignorance, so Isaiah declared, flourishes in the soil of rebellion against the Holy One. When personal experiential knowledge of God is lacking, ungodliness claims the lives of people (Rom. 1:18-22). Ignorance of this sort directed Jesus' enemies to crucify Him.

Two aspects of this ignorance call for attention:

1. There was ignorance concerning Jesus' nature and mission. Even His closest disciples had difficulty in understanding Him and realizing His true purpose on earth. Small wonder, then, that men driven by hate and envy failed to grasp His mind and mission. Hate-filled eyes seldom see the worth of a person.

Had Israel's leaders accepted Jesus' Messiahship, they probably would have accepted His judgment of them. Instead, they were angry with Him because He showed up their moral failures, their distorted vision and limited perspectives, and their prevalent hypocrisies. Their proud refusal to admit spiritual blindness demonstrated their guilt (John 9:39-41). There is none so blind as he who will not see even when confronted by clear evidence. Jesus' critics were like a woman who lost an argument to her husband. Said he: "She agreed that I was right, but she was never convinced about it!"

An opponent may be reduced to silence, as Jesus' enemies often were, but that does not mean the opponent accepts the truth of another's position. In spite of His amazing miracles and clear religious teachings, Jesus' critics called Him a false prophet, an imposter, a friend of Satan. They resorted to an old trick: if you can't refute the logic, discredit the logician. Refusal to change one's mind when change is warranted by the facts closes the door to new truth and leaves one trapped in ignorance.

In a sense, Jesus' enemies did know what they were doing. They were resisting change in the status quo. Jesus was endangering the religious establishment, threatening to give religion and worship back to the common people. Caiaphas, the high priest, saw Jesus as a challenge to existing ecclesiastical authority. The issue for him was clear: Kill the opposition and save the establishment (John 11:49-50). Fanatical zeal reaches its peak in misguided religious people who dogmatically affirm their actions as God's will. Caiaphas and the Jewish hierarchy knew what they were doing. Even so, their actions belonged to that ignorance of which the prophets wrote.

This is clear from the apostolic preaching which gave interpretation to Jesus' death. Peter pointed the finger accusingly at the persons responsible for the crucifixion. "You handed him over to be killed, and you disowned him before Pilate, . . . You killed the author of life." Then he added, "Now, brothers, I know that you acted in ignorance, as did your leaders" (Acts 3:15,17). A similar observation occurred in Paul's letter to the Corinthians. Earthly leaders, he noted, lack knowledge of the divine wisdom at work in the world. "None of the rulers of this age understood it, for if they had, they would not have crucified the Lord of glory" (1 Cor. 2:8). Paul himself had once sought to destroy the Christian movement, acting, as he confessed, "in ignorance and unbelief" (1 Tim. 1:13).

2. Their ignorance caused them to miss the significance of Jesus' death. The best of minds across the ages have failed to grasp the full meaning of Calvary. How could those persons responsible for the crucifixion know what they were doing or how God would turn that cruel cross into an instrument of salvation?

Calvary, after all, was God's love in operation. There God was in Christ reconciling the world to Himself (2 Cor. 5:19). To the world, death on a cross meant shame and degradation, a stumbling block to Jews and sheer folly to Gentiles (1 Cor. 1:23). Even Israel's religious leaders failed to see suffering love as redemptive. Would God let His chosen One endure such humiliation? God, they felt, would show His real nature in *power.* So let that man come down from the cross if He was indeed God's Son! The full meaning and mystery of the cross was lost to them.

Calvary's real contest was between righteousness and evil, love and hate, heaven and hell. At the cross, said George Buttrick, "heaven met evil's power in dread encounter and conquered in love's seeming defeat." The world derisively called Him "Jesus of Nazareth, King of the Jews." That was the best ignorant men could do. But the testimony of the ages is that Jesus Christ is King of kings and Lord of lords.

Conquering Evil

Forgiveness of sin signifies the destruction of evil. Vengeance and retaliation keep evil alive. Jesus' method of meeting evil differed from the psalmist who called on God to rid the earth of the sinner and the sin (Ps. 55:15; 94:1-3; 137:7-9; 94:1-13). Jesus was concerned for the rescue of the individual. He never asked God to ignore the guilt and the wickedness of His enemies. But behind their wretched conduct, Jesus saw persons in need of God. He was moved by their need even more than His own. So He interceded for them, imploring God to forgive them.

Sin, Jesus knew, ultimately is a blow at God Himself. Furthermore, God alone can forgive sin and rescue sinners. That is why Jesus represented the prodigal son as saying, "I have sinned against heaven" (Luke 15:21). Centuries before, a penitent man had prayed toward God, "Against you, you only, have I sinned/and done what is evil in your sight" (Ps. 51:4). There is forgiveness waiting for persons who pray like that. Whatever else the Bible teaches, it consistently declares that God loves us and meets our penitence with forgiveness and acceptance. Is there anything greater in this vast universe than such love?

A Chicago paper carried the story of an orphan lad and his adoption. While in the orphanage, the boy had known the love and kindly care of a woman whose heart was big enough to embrace many homeless children. Despite crowded conditions and limited facilities, the boy had found security and affection. To win him over, his adoptive mother described all the varied comforts, toys, and gadgets that awaited him in his new home. He listened politely and then asked a question that weighed heavily on his little heart. "Will you love a fellow?"

That is what we ask of God: "Could you love even me?" The answer comes back immediately: "God so loved the world that he gave his one and only Son, that whoever believes in him shall not perish but have eternal life" (John 3:16). The Man on the cross is His Son. He hangs there above persons but below God, as though trying to bring the two together.

"Father, forgive them, for they do not know what they are doing." Was there ever such a prayer before or since? Carlyle was correct. Those are the sublimest words ever uttered. Their impact was felt immediately. A hardened criminal on a cross nearby was deeply moved by Jesus' intercession for His enemies. He opened up his life to the Master in that moment.

Can you imagine the results in today's world should a sizable number of Jesus' followers adopt His example in handling evil? As taught and exemplified by Jesus, the forgiving spirit meets evil with goodness and so ends evil's domination. The way of forgiveness has not been tried and found wanting. For many, it has been tried, found difficult, and not tried again. Despite that fact, Jesus' insistence on forgiveness still remains the most striking innovation in morality ever given humankind.

10

The Vigil of Prayer
Ephesians 6: 18-20; 1 Timothy 2: 1

According to James Smart, Christians live in an embattled situation. We work, worship, and pray within the context of perpetual struggle. As children of God we experience special joy and receive many benefits. But our lives are never immune to stress, conflict, pain, and grief.

In describing the Christian pilgrimage, Paul drew many of his descriptive terms from military life. The believer is like a soldier. He belongs to an army, is under command, receives equipment for the contest, and constantly faces a fierce enemy. Not by accident did the old warrior of the cross list prayer as a part of the Christian soldier's equipment for battle. "Pray in the Spirit on all occasions with all kinds of prayers and requests. With this in mind, be alert and always keep on praying for all the saints" (v. 18). When the enemy assaults you, Paul urged, launch a counterattack of prayer.

Continuity of Prayer

Life would be a jumbled mess if people literally obeyed the biblical command to "Pray without ceasing" (1 Thess. 5:16, KJV). It would be infinitely better, however, if persons accepted prayer as the permanent posture of the soul toward God and lived accordingly. The call to constancy in prayer (Luke 18:1; Rom. 12:12; Phil. 4:6; Col. 4:2; 1 Thess. 5:17) does not prevent us from doing the world's needful work. Nor should that work preempt prayer.

"Pray . . . on all occasions." Every incident of life (*kairos*) can be brought before God when we pray. Forget the notion that God is too busy to be bothered with our prayers. If we hold a personal relationship

85

with Him, we can talk freely with Him about all the things that concern our lives. Prayer after all is "a living voice speaking to a living ear."

Why is the Bible so insistent on constancy in prayer? For one thing, *spasmodic or infrequent praying is powerless and ineffective.* Christians who seldom pray miss the blessedness of fellowship with God and the divine energy that He pumps through the soul. They are weak in spirit. Worship is unappetizing and boring for them. If God's work is done by a praying people, then prayerless persons impede that work. How different things are when the lines of communication are regularly open to God!

Some people pray only when emergencies or crises arise. They turn toward God when critical illness or other grave troubles invade their lives. For them, prayer is a spare tire to be used when life goes flat. In Shakespeare's drama *The Tempest,* the sailors cry out amid the storm, "To prayers! To prayers! All is lost!" That calls to mind an oft-heard remark, "When you can't do anything else, you can pray."

Certainly, periods of stress and unexpected crises are times for praying. But prayer in advance of crises, prayer as a daily discipline, will prepare us for any event that comes. Prayer keeps oil in life's lamp, making us ready when the midnight hour descends upon us (Matt. 25:1-12).

Because of our human weakness we need to pray at all times. The robust Christian warrior is one who prays constantly. Prayer focuses the mind on God, sets one in the ways of righteousness, and positions one on the firing line. "Be strong in the Lord and in his mighty power" (Eph. 6:10). Those who wait upon the Lord find strength in times of weakness. They are renewed each day. The power God pours into their souls teaches them to cope with life in the fast lane or endure the slow pace attended by drudgery and dullness (Isa. 40:31).

The desperate need of the world makes constancy in prayer imperative. How else can we face a world that is sick at heart, full of ruthlessness, alienated from God, and facing His judgment? Christians cannot live aloof from the cruelty, poverty, and fear that tear human lives apart. Millions live with anxiety and uncertainty about the future. The "man come of age" has created a world full of scientific and technological wonders and at the same time one filled with unimaginable horrors. Terrorism stalks our cities, crime is rampant in the land, and the threat of nuclear destruction hangs over our heads. Can we face all these apart from the divine help that comes through prayer? This is the world in which we are to witness and minister in Christ's name. Like Jesus' disciples, we have a twofold task: to pray and to work (John 15:7-8). These must never be separated if we are to reach our world for Him.

The persistent presence of the evil one necessitates constancy in prayer. From Jesus we learn the value of prayer as a defense against Satan's tricks. He struggled through prayer against the desires of the flesh which counseled withdrawal from the battle. He resisted the subtleties of Satan which pointed His mind to easier ways of achieving God's will (see Matt. 4:1-11). One thing is clear: Jesus never questioned the reality of the devil. Nor should we. We need the full armor of God, of which prayer is a part, to resist the "powers of this dark world" which seek to entrap us.

Simon Peter, once so vulnerable to Satan's devices (Mark 8:33; Luke 22:31-32), gave sound advice when he wrote, "Be self-controlled and alert. Your enemy the devil prowls around like a roaring lion looking for someone to devour. Resist him, standing firm in the faith" (1 Pet. 5:8-9). How better to resist him than from our knees?

> My soul, be on thy guard,
> Ten thousand foes arise;
> The hosts of sin are pressing hard
> To draw thee from the skies.
>
> O watch, and fight, and pray,
> The battle ne'er give o'er;
> Renew it boldly every day,
> And help divine implore.

Comprehensiveness in Prayer

Prayer employs a variety of forms. "Pray . . . with all kinds of prayers and requests." These forms, rightly used, serve the essential purpose of prayer: "communication between ourselves as personal beings and God, the heavenly Father, as the ultimate personal reality in the universe."[1]

Comprehensive praying allows both form and freedom. We do not have to choose one or the other. Sincerity and genuineness are neither guaranteed by impromptu prayers nor destroyed by planned ones. When we pray "in the Spirit" there is liberty. Such praying, however, may employ those historic forms used by Christians across the ages (see 1 Tim. 2:1).

1. There is the prayer of confession. The repentant soul gains an audience with God. "If I had cherished sin in my heart," the psalmist declared, "the Lord would not have listened;/but God has surely listened/and heard my voice in prayer" (Ps. 66:18-19). Confession grows out of a lively sense of God which in turn produces in us a consciousness of sin and guilt (Isa. 59:2; Luke 5:8). It calls for complete honesty, the readiness to acknowledge our personal inadequacies and our specific sins—not a recitation of vague generalities. Our pride and disposition to sin make confession mandatory. Confession is thus a perennial need. It opens the life to divine forgiveness and moral renewal (1 John 1:9; Ps. 32:1-5).

2. There is the prayer of thanksgiving. Ingratitude is one of the basest sins, yet it rules many lives. Thanksgiving acknowledges God as the source of life and all benefits. It recognizes our reliance upon the good earth and remembers our dependence upon others. Paul thus admonished us to let "thanksgiving be made for everyone" (1 Tim. 2:1). We are bound up with others in the bundle of life and owe so much to so many.

Gratitude grows by expressing it. Often this can be done by small deeds that keep others aware of our true feelings. I know a man who, as long as his mother lived, wrote her a card each day. He exemplified the truth that cultivation of thanksgiving ensures its growth.

3. There is the prayer of petition. Petition is not an inferior form of praying. Its legitimacy is well attested by Scripture and the practice of God's people. Paul, for example, urged the Philippian Christians to make wise and frequent use of petition. "In everything, by prayer and petition, with thanksgiving, present your requests to God" (Phil. 4:6).

Supplication or petition grows out of a recognition of personal need, our own or that of others. It is emboldened by the belief that God can supply that need, that He indeed knows about it even before we ask (Matt. 6:32).

4. There is the prayer of intercession. Intercession really is a form of supplication, a petition offered on behalf of another person or other persons and events.[2] The great intercessory prayers of the Bible are concerned principally with emotional, mental, and spiritual needs (Gen. 18:23-33; Num. 14:13-19; John 17; Eph. 3:14-21). Paul's frequent prayers for the churches, reflected in his letters, further illustrate this fact. Praying for material blessings is legitimate, for God is concerned about our total welfare. But the burden of biblical intercession deals with higher priorities.

Intercession is a vital part of Jesus' high priestly ministry (Heb. 7:23-24). It belongs to our ministry also. Intercessory prayer has several values: It focuses our attention upon the specific needs of individuals; it strengthens those whose concerns we share; it is a way of cooperating with God in the achievement of His purposes.

P. T. Forsyth saw intercessory prayer as the best corrective for a critical, grumbling spirit.[3] Praying for others cleanses our souls. It also affects the attitudes and actions of others. A pastor learned this in dealing with a hostile church member. This woman was habitually late for worship. She always made a dramatic entry, showing off her expensive garments, disturbing other worshipers, and greatly irritating the pastor. The pastor considered several ways to check her annoying behavior. Finally, he decided to make her an object of prayer. For weeks he prayed for her, confessing his own irritation as well as her irreverence. Then one morning as the worship began, he saw her sitting quietly in the pew. She was never again a problem.

Alertness at Prayer

Prayer retreats are not an end in themselves. They are most useful if we return from them refreshed and empowered, ready to meet the problems and complexities of daily living. The admonition to "be alert and always keep on praying" envisions perpetual struggle. Like the ancient watchman upon the city wall, the Christian soldier maintains a steady vigil. He wears his armor well, but he also keeps fully awake. A sleeping warrior is little protection for a city and no threat to the enemy.

The call to alertness suggests waiting, watchfulness, and sometimes struggle. The vigil of prayer for Jacob was like wrestling with God. For Jesus, it was the tears and sweat of Gethsemane. Praying is more than a pleasant pastime. Have you ever grappled with the issues involved in some decision, seeking God's guidance through extensive praying? Have you ever battled with an evil desire, prayed endlessly for a lost soul, agonized over a situation that seemed beyond solution? Then you know how intense prayer can be.

Vigilance in prayer is made necessary by the unrelenting foe we face. Satan would break our spirits and destroy our relationship with God but for our prayers. There is never a time when we can lower our guard. Every stage of life brings its own special brand of temptation.

> Ne'er think the victory won,
> Nor lay thine armor down;
> The work of faith will not be done,
> Till thou obtain the crown.

The vigil of prayer calls for perseverance. "Always keep on praying." Persistent praying, when done in the Spirit, deepens our consciousness of God and makes us more reliant upon Him. It enables us to meet the cynicism which questions God's reality and disparages prayer's worth. It helps us counter the acids of secularism which eat away at Christian faith.

Mature believers keep praying even when God seems hidden or silent. Thoughtful Christians do not drop the prayer habit when prayers go unanswered. If wise, they will analyze the possible causes of their prayer failures. A ten-year-old boy prayed fervently for his favorite baseball team, the New York Yankees. He had heard in Sunday School that God always answers our prayers. The struggling Yankees, however, lost the pennant drive and the young lad lost his confidence in Sunday school teachers and prayer. Said he, "I promised God I would do anything, even become a preacher, if He would let the Yankees win. But they lost. I'm never going to pray again!"

That reaction is understandable in children, but it hardly befits adults. Adults should realize that God delays some answers to prayer, responds at other times in ways we hardly expect, and denies some requests altogether. Our prayers are plagued by human fallibility. God's responses reflect His sovereign grace.

"Keep on praying." Include "all the saints," known and unknown to you. This accords with Jesus' statement about praying for the coming of the kingdom and the doing of God's will on earth (Matt. 6:10). The fulfilment of that purpose requires human effort coupled with divine power. In effect, it means praying for the church, the people of God on mission for Him, and all those through whom God is at work in today's world. "Intercession includes others in the dialogue of devotion."[4]

Paul's humanity appears in his urgent plea that his readers pray regularly for him. He was finite, vulnerable, and in prison. But he did not ask for release or an easier life. Paul's primary concern was for the progress of the gospel. He desired three things: (1) an open mouth filled with well-chosen words; (2) a grasp of the mystery of the gospel in relation to human need; and (3) courage to declare that gospel in the face of adversity.

Ministers and missionaries still face those needs that Paul felt, and they merit our constant supplication in their behalf. Our prayers, however, must range over the totality of human need, including all kinds and conditions of persons (2 Tim. 2:1-11). Neglect of that vigilance in prayer is sin.

Prayer helps one master the weakness of the flesh and bring it in line with the willingness of the spirit (Matt. 26:41). It keeps Christian soldiers alert and energetic for battle. Confronted by the enemy, they don the gospel armor, putting on each piece with prayer. Prayer keeps them alert, sensitive to the Commander's orders and ready to obey.

> I do not ask that Thou shalt front the fray,
>   And drive the warring foeman from my sight;
> I only ask, O Lord, by night, by day,
>   Strength for the fight.
>
> When foes upon me press, let me not quail,
>   Nor think to turn me into coward flight.
> I only ask, to make my arms prevail,
>   Strength for the fight![5]

Notes

Chapter 1

1. Georgia Harkness, *The Providence of God* (Nashville: Abingdon Press, 1960), p. 122.
2. The Holy Bible, *New International Version* Copyright © 1978 by New York International Bible Society. Unless otherwise indicated, Scripture quotations herein are from this translation.
3. D. R. Sharpe, *Walter Rauschenbusch* (New York: The Macmillan Company, 1942), pp. 451-452.
4. Fisher Humphreys, *The Heart of Prayer* (Nashville: Broadman Press, 1980), p. 11.

Chapter 2

1. John I. Durham, "Psalms," *The Broadman Bible Commentary* (Nashville: Broadman Press, 1971), vol. 4, p. 275.
2. Rudyard Kipling, "Recessional" in *1,000 Quotable Poems* (Chicago: Willett, Clark & Company, 1937), vol. 1, p. 42.

Chapter 3

1. W. R. Taylor, "Psalms," *Interpreter's Bible* (Nashville: Abingdon Press, 1955), vol. 4, p. 169.
2. Kipling, "Recessional" in *1,000 Quotable Poems* (Chicago: Willett, Clark & Company, 1937), n.p.u.

Chapter 4

1. Cited in Gerald Heard, *A Preface to Prayer* (New York: Harper & Brothers, 1944), p. 172.
2. Peter Chew, *The Inner World of the Middle-Aged Man* (New York: Macmillan Company, 1976), p. 5.
3. Ibid., pp. 4-7.

4. Ibid., p. 116.

5. Gail Sheehy, *Passages* (New York: E. P. Dutton & Company, 1976), p. 257.

Chapter 5

1. Walter Rauschenbusch, *For God and the People* (Chicago: The Pilgrim Press, 1910), p. 15.

2. Karl Barth, *Prayer* (Philadelphia: Westminster Press, 1952), p. 45.

3. Ernst Lohmeyer, *"Our Father"* (New York: Harper & Row, 1965), p. 75.

4. Walter Lüthi, *The Lord's Prayer* (Richmond, Va.: John Knox Press, 1961), p. 24.

5. Ibid., p. 43.

6. Frank Stagg, "Matthew," *The Broadman Bible Commentary,* ed. Clifton Allen (Nashville: Broadman Press, 1969), vol. 8, p. 116.

7. Lüthi, *Broadman Commentary,* pp. 58-59.

8. Lohmeyer, *"Our Father,"* p. 231.

Chapter 6

1. Reinhold Niebuhr, *Does Civilization Need Religion?* (New York: Macmillan Company, 1927), p. 12.

2. George A. Buttrick, *Prayer* (Nashville: Abingdon-Cokesbury Press, 1942), pp. 115-118.

3. Oswald J. Smith, "Then Jesus Came," in *Foursquare Hymnal,* published by Rodeheaver Hall-Mack Company, 1957, p. 237.

4. Buttrick, *Prayer,* pp. 154-155.

5. T. W. Manson, *The Beginning of the Gospel* (London: Oxford University Press, 1950), p. 63.

6. Eduard Schweizer, *The Good News According to Mark* (Atlanta: John Knox Press, 1976), p. 188.

Chapter 7

1. John Baillie, *The Sense of the Presence of God* (London: Oxford University Press, 1962), p. 236.

2. George A. Buttrick, "Luke," *Interpreter's Bible* (Nashville: Abingdon-Cokesbury Press, 1952), vol. 8, p. 298.

3. Ray Summers, *Commentary on Luke* (Waco: Word Books, 1972), pp. 200-201.

4. Albert E. Bailey, *The Gospel in Hymns* (New York: Charles Scribner's Sons, 1950), pp. 322-323.

Chapter 8

1. George Foot Moore, *Judaism* (Cambridge, Mass.: Harvard University Press, 1946), 3 vols.

2. J. H. F. Peile, *The Reproach of the Gospel* (New York: Longmans, Green, and Company, 1909), pp. 155-156.

3. H. E. Luccock, *Studies in the Parables of Jesus* (New York: Abingdon Press, 1917), p. 98.

4. Luccock, *Parables of Jesus,* p. 100.

5. Joachim Jeremias, *The Parables of Jesus* (New York: Charles Scribner's Sons, 1955), pp. 114-115.

Chapter 9

1. Cited by F. C. Grant, *Christ's Victory and Ours* (New York: Macmillan Company, 1951), p. 12.

2. L. H. Marshall, *The Challenge of New Testament Ethics* (New York: Macmillan & Company Ltd., 1956), p. 96.

Chapter 10

1. Glenn Hinson, *The Reaffirmation of Prayer* (Nashville: Broadman Press, 1979), p. 10.

2. Ibid., p. 95.

3. P. T. Forsyth, *The Soul of Prayer* (Grand Rapids, Mich.: William B. Eerdmans, 1916), p. 77.

4. Dale Moody, *The Word of Truth* (Grand Rapids, Mich.: William B. Eerdmans, 1981), p. 158.

5. Paul Lawrence Dunbar, "A Warrior's Prayer," from *Masterpieces of Religious Verse,* ed. James Dalton (Nashville: Broadman Press, 1948), p. 437.